Success in College

From C's in High School to A's in College

PETER F. BURNS

Published in partnership with the
National Society of Collegiate Scholars

ROWMAN & LITTLEFIELD EDUCATION
Lanham, Maryland • Toronto • Oxford
2006

Published in partnership with the
National Society of Collegiate Scholars

Published in the United States of America
by Rowman & Littlefield Education
A Division of Rowman & Littlefield Publishers, Inc.
A wholly owned subsidiary of The Rowman & Littlefield Publishing Group, Inc.
4501 Forbes Boulevard, Suite 200, Lanham, Maryland 20706
www.rowmaneducation.com

PO Box 317
Oxford
OX2 9RU, UK

British Library Cataloguing in Publication Information Available

Library of Congress Cataloging-in-Publication Data
Burns, Peter F.
  Success in college : from C's in high school to A's in college / Peter F. Burns.
     p. cm.
  "Published in partnership with the National Society of Collegiate Scholars."
  Includes bibliographical references.
  ISBN-13: 978-1-57886-458-4 (hardcover : alk. paper)
  ISBN-10: 1-57886-458-5 (hardcover : alk. paper)
  ISBN-13: 978-1-57886-459-1 (pbk. : alk. paper)
  ISBN-10: 1-57886-459-3 (pbk. : alk. paper)
  1. College student orientation—United States. 2. Study skills. I. Title.
LB2343.32.B87 2006
378.1'980973—dc22
                                                              2006002918

™ The paper used in this publication meets the minimum requirements of
American National Standard for Information Sciences—Permanence of
Paper for Printed Library Materials, ANSI/NISO Z39.48-1992.
Manufactured in the United States of America.

Contents

Introduction

The Purpose of This Book: You Can Make College a Learning Experience

My introduction to grain alcohol was painful. The night before my college career was to begin, a friend from high school threw a grain-alcohol party in his dorm room. The so-called punch, which was served in a large garbage can, was roughly 99 percent 200-proof alcohol and 1 percent red dye #2, but it tasted like Hawaiian Punch. How bad could it be?

Bad!

As another high school friend and I walked back to her dorm after the party, the grain alcohol not only punched her; it knocked her out. One second she was talking and walking; the next she was mumbling in the fetal position. The transformation occurred instantaneously. The campus was so large and we were so new to it that we had no clue how to get to her dorm. After starting and stopping on many occasions, we made it to the library, which was close to my friend's dorm.

I got to my dorm room at a reasonable hour, about 1 A.M., and I went to bed feeling all right, but I did not sleep long. I woke up at about 3 A.M. and the bed was spinning and I was sweating profusely. The punch delivered another knockout. Quickly, I jumped from the top bunk and landed on my roommate, whose bed was in the middle of the room. The overcrowding at the university turned rooms for two (or doubles) into triples, and three people lived in our room. As I fell on him, Tom, who would be my college roommate for the next two and a half years and my friend for life, exclaimed, "Jesus Christ!" I hurried into the bathroom and vomited.

As I knelt there puking, I remember shaking my head. I had vowed to transform myself from a class clown and mediocre student in high school to a responsible *student* in college, but here I sat kissing the porcelain god on night number 1. As I left the bathroom, I knew I needed to get my act together quickly, and I did. The first lesson I learned from this incident was that college and high school life differed. I could never stay out that late *and* get drunk on a school night in high school. Next, I had the discipline and the will to get out of bed the next morning, to attend all my classes that day, and to even make baseball practice.[1] One of the most important things that you need to understand about college is that you must make it to class, even if you have a hangover. If you are enough of an adult to party all night, then you should be enough of an adult to get up the next day. If you cannot attend class after partying all night, then do not stay out all night. Finally, I learned that college presented many traps and distractions, and if I was to flourish, then I needed to make academics—and not grain alcohol—my priority.

If you are enough of an adult to party all night, then you should be enough of an adult to get up the next day.

Some sixteen years later, I am a college professor, who, to the best of my recollection, drank grain alcohol one more time, and that was ugly too. Determination, discipline, and some intelligence enabled me to make that transformation from a very average high school student to an inductee into many honor societies in college. I learned many great lessons about how to succeed in college, and I want to use this book to impart some of the most important information and advice to you.

MY MEDIOCRITY

It is hard for me to communicate how mediocre I really was in high school. Let's see if a few stories help make my case. After earning my first master's degree, I tutored a family friend, Brian, whom I had not seen in ten years. Brian was a junior in high school and I was twenty-three. Brian reminded me of myself. He was smart but lazy. His parents cared deeply about his progress and his performance, but he didn't. Brian is one of the nicest people you could ever meet. He has a million-dollar personality, but he did not apply himself.

Because we had not seen each other in so long, Brian expected to be tutored by Mr. Nerd. He did not think I would relate to him or to his troubles in school. Quickly, he found out how wrong he was. During our first session, I explained to Brian that I knew every lazy trick in the book. I told him that we were similar in high school. I didn't study hard; he didn't study hard. I didn't pay attention; he didn't pay attention. Fooling around was my priority; fooling around was his priority.

At one point during our sessions, Brian admitted that he had misjudged me. He thought I would not understand his plight because I was supersmart and I was always a great student. I told him that both statements were false. I am not superintelligent. I am not dumb, but I was certainly not the smartest student in high school, college, or graduate school, and I am not nearly the smartest person in my profession. My success emanates from *some intelligence* and *a ton of hard work*. I explained to Brian that he could never expect to do well if he did not listen or read.

I rarely studied in high school. The night before the test, I may have looked at the book and the notes, but then again, on many occasions, I just winged it. My English teacher, who met individually with the students to discuss their grades, asked me whether I studied and blanked during the tests or if I did not study and consequently did not know the answers. Most often, I did not know the answer because I did not prepare.

I just did not care. My grades improved from time to time because I could not stand the punishment from my parents. For the most part, however, I didn't care. I could not and did not motivate myself to improve in high school. As I say throughout this book, if *you* don't want to learn, then no one can make you.

My priority in high school was to entertain. I really wanted people to like me, and therefore I would entertain them. In my senior year, I took accounting, and I was terrific—not in my academic performance but in my entertaining performance. At the beginning of each class, the teacher assigned an exercise that the students needed to complete during that period. I rarely finished the exercises. Instead, I either talked to the teacher, who became my friend, or I performed a stand-up comedy routine in class.[2] I entertained the class as the students worked on their assignments. I am not kidding. At the end of each class, I received the answers from my friends. The teacher knew there was no way I could have done the exercises on my own, and he gave me a D for the course.

My best performances took place in the high school library. During our free period, students could get a pass to go to the library. In my classes, I would think about ways to create chaos in the library. Freshmen through seniors came to the library and these study periods were my time to shine. At the time, I was quite pleased that I received four full-year bans from the library during my high school career. These two stories illustrate my class clown tendencies, but in many classes, I simply did nothing. On a regular basis, I either doodled, fell asleep, or asked for a bathroom pass.

My first high school report card was especially unforgettable. To the best of my memory, I received one B, four C's, and a D.[3] Literally, my mother needed to sit down after she saw the report card. Then she asked, "Is that a D I see?" The thoughts of that day and those words still make me ill. Unfortunately, I think my mother saw at least two more D's during my high school years, but she came to expect but never accept mediocrity. Overall, my high school report cards had plenty of B's and C's, but not many A's. The accumulation of A's and the elimination of C's came when I reached college.

College is an overwhelming experience, for which most students are not prepared. No high school, not even a college preparatory school or elite boarding school, prepares students completely for the college experience. The freedom, demands, and social climate of university life are not easily simulated.

Success in College provides straightforward advice and basic information on the most important factors that affect learning and grades. After I graduated from college, I received a PhD, and I have been a professor for the last seven years. My experiences as a professor and adviser supported what I learned as a student and provided additional insight into what it takes to learn and achieve good grades in college. I impart these lessons in this book.

WHY ME?

Why should you listen to me? Unlike many professors, at one time or another, I have been the best, the worst, and the most mediocre student in a class. To say I underachieved in high school is an understatement. In a recent survey, one-third of high school students claimed they goofed off with their friends whereas nearly 40 percent neither paid attention nor worked very hard.[4] I relate to these findings. Basically, I blew off my high school studies. One day during my sophomore year in high school, my sister and her friend, both graduates of a private high school and college students at the time, picked me up after school. My sister's friend was amazed that I left school with no book bag, no books, and no folder . . . nothing. I did not apply myself and my grades reflected this fact.

To say the least, my class rank and high school GPA were unspectacular. I never made the honor roll in high school. During the last few weeks of my senior year in high school, Mr. Germe, a no-nonsense, barrel-chested teacher, took two of my friends and me to his office for coffee and a discussion. Mr. Germe cared. He asked why I wanted to attend college. I told him that the women in my hometown were lame. I was going to the University of Connecticut (UConn) to meet real women. Yes, I was delusional. I also told Mr. Germe that I wanted to party. My answer aggravated Mr. Germe, who responded, "No, no, no." Mr. Germe suggested strongly that I not waste my parents' money by attending college. Instead, his plan called for me to work in the brass factory in town. As he explained it, I could party and meet women at the bar every Saturday night. Mr. Germe's strategy even allowed me to make money whereas my plan called for significant spending. He said I should go to college only if I wanted to learn. Mr. Germe concluded his talk by advising me not to unpack my bags when I went to UConn because I would last no longer than one semester. To this day, I do not know whether he was serious or he was simply motivating. Whatever his intent, Mr. Germe helped light a fire that still burns.

Research says, "Students have three motives for attending college"[5]:

1. Instrumental—students want degrees for social and economic mobility

2. Scholastic—students want intellectual stimulation

3. Social—students want to enjoy the extracurricular life that college offers

---

Shortly after Mr. Germe's talk, I was in the office of one of the guidance counselors at my high school. Have you noticed that I was not in class much during the final days of my senior year? As the guidance counselor and I held our discussion, a member of the National Honor Society walked in, and she told me to leave because, as a member of the National Honor Society, she took priority over me. I remember looking at her and thinking, "This will never happen again. I will never lose out because I did not try." She made the National Honor Society because she tried, and I did not. In the future, I thought, she would have to beat me at my best in order to finish ahead of me. I can sleep at night if people perform better when I try my best. This was not the case in high school.

I never forgot these events, which provided some of the desire I needed to work hard. Consequently, I paid close attention to anyone who told stories about college. Over the years, I collected these experiences. The lessons I learned from these stories helped me write this book.

My experiences taught me that *effort*, rather than sheer intelligence, constitutes the key ingredient to learning and high grades. Students need that desire to excel. Desire is vital. When I went to college, I wanted good grades. You are mistaken to believe that intelligence alone determines grades. The rare student excels without trying. For the most part, those who dedicate time to and devise strategies for learning are the most successful. I hope these lessons facilitate the learning process for you or someone about whom you care.

Effort rather than sheer intelligence constitutes the key ingredient to learning and high grades.

The attention I paid to excelling during my college career enabled me to write this book. When I was in college, I focused upon getting good grades. In fact, you could say I obsessed over it. My college experience qualifies me to provide advice about university life as a student. Furthermore, I am young enough to remember most of my college experience.

Research says, "Motivation strongly affects GPAs."[6]

Another basis for my opinions comes from observations of countless college students at several universities. I served as a teaching assistant at two large research institutions and I taught full-time at a small, elite liberal arts college and a Jesuit university. As a professor, I spend a great deal of time advising students. I offer suggestions and guidance to all my students. At the end of each course, I tell students that they are now my former students, which entitles them to come to my office to receive advice about school. My advising extends well beyond the students assigned to me. I use my formal and informal advising sessions to teach about study habits, graduate school, and attitudes about education. My advising duties provide me with greater insight into how to handle the college experience. My advisees' experiences serve as another basis for the advice I offer in this book.

My experiences suggest that many students are ill prepared for university life. Some students arrive with no expectations. They have not considered what is ahead of them. Others, who do ponder what is in store for them, believe that high school and college are relatively similar. They are not. Members of another group, of which I was a part, understand that college is a new frontier but they have no idea what this experience entails. I asked my sister, friends, coworkers, and others with college experience what to expect. Their advice was invaluable but limited.

Success in College is not only designed to guide incoming students. Many college students can improve and learn more even if they already maintain high GPAs. The advice and information contained throughout the book can improve the learning experiences of all students. No student understands all aspects of learning and the information and recommendations on goals, expectations, preparation, the semester, professors, studying, writing papers, and other topics can enrich the learning and academic experience of students in all years of college.

To me, success in college means good grades *and* learning. This book offers suggestions about what to expect from college, how to prepare mentally, and how to approach each semester. It also focuses upon study habits, note taking, writing papers, studying for exams, working with your professors, class conduct, advising, and assessing your performance. I use my experiences as a student, teaching assistant, and professor to give practical advice about how to do your best in school. Before you read on, I must tell you that college takes great preparation, time, and effort. No one can tell you how much time it will take to learn. You need to determine that through your experiences, but you must be prepared to dedicate significant amounts of time and your life to your studies.

"What about enjoying what one's learning? Could this not be included in definitions of success?"

—former student

I discussed earlier versions of this book with many colleagues and former students. Two people in particular, one a former student and the other a colleague and friend, remarked that I missed one important goal of college—you need to find subjects you like, study them, and enjoy what you are learning. They were correct. You should be passionate about the subjects you study.

A successful college experience includes finding subjects of interest to you and enjoying what you learn.

Students should use their college years to pursue subjects of great interest to them. College provides an excellent venue to explore your intellectual curiosity. Students should take classes in a number of different fields to see what interests them. One time on National Public Radio (NPR), I heard a young professional say, "Do what you like and the money will follow you." I agree. You should select a major according to what interests you. Too many students pick majors that allow them to make the most money even though they prefer other subjects. Quality of life should matter to you and working in a profession that does not excite you will negatively affect your outlook regardless of how much money you earn.

I wrote this book partly for the present-day equivalent of that eighteen-year-old Pete Burns, who feared college. I also wrote this book for those who think high school and college are similar but have no clue that college economics, physics, math, and English differ drastically from high school classes of the same titles. I also wrote this book for parents, who put unrealistic expectations on their college-bound children. This book allows parents to offer solid advice and enables them to detect warning signs that their children are either not ready for college or are struggling in a particular semester or school year.

This book provides no shortcuts. The first and last rule is that you must work hard. If you do not prepare, attend class, study, read, and learn on a consistent basis, then no advice will help you. The suggestions and information in this book help those who want to succeed and are prepared to work hard in order to accomplish this goal.

Others say, "Through the shared experiences of more than 30 years in higher education, many of our observations point to a chronic apathetic attitude, which breeds behavior that impedes academic success."[7]

Throughout the book, I offer concrete rules for success in college. These rules are not personal preferences but instead include tactics and strategies that I believe to be essential for learning and achieving higher grades. Hard work and consistent preparation are two such rules.

At other times, I provide general tips about how to succeed in college. With regard to note taking, for example, my general tip is to develop a system that allows you to take comprehensive and accurate notes. Writing on the right side of the notebook allowed me to accomplish these goals. Whereas your personal preference may be to write on both sides of your notebook, the general point is that you need to develop a system that allows you to take copious notes. At the end of each chapter, I provide a summary of the concrete rules and general tips I offer for the subject of that chapter.

In each chapter, I summarize and quote from studies on the topics I cover. I did not research these topics until *after* I wrote my story. These short summations, which appear throughout the chapters, complement and supplement the information and advice I offer. I agree with the findings and advice presented in these summaries.

The next two chapters focus upon the purpose of college and how to prepare for and what to expect from this university experience. Other chapters concentrate upon study habits, college papers and exams, your professors, advising, proper classroom behavior, and how to evaluate your performance. The final chapters compare the general characteristics of good and not-so-good students, offer advice to parents, and summarize the most vital information and advice I provide in this book.

College is so important. My experiences in college shaped the person I am today. They taught me more about the value of hard work and attention to detail. My college years allowed me to develop self-discipline and they facilitated my confidence and maturity.

My studies also made me a more informed citizen and a better person. As a result of learning, I understand the causes and consequences of things in my personal and professional lives. Knowledge and critical thinking lead to power. After you read *Success in College*, I hope that you will be better positioned to learn and to achieve good grades. I also want you to understand how important hard work is for life in general, and for college in particular.

Why are you in college? Mr. Germe asked a similar question when I was in high school and ultimately I concluded that grades and learning were my reasons. I ask this question of many students with whom I come into contact. I see too many undergraduates fail to maximize their college experiences. They come to college, study when they must, and neither learn nor receive the grades they are capable of earning. This book encourages you to understand why you are in college and then it provides advice and information that allows you to take full advantage of this wonderful opportunity.

Who Is Dr. Peter Burns?[8]

1. Mediocre high school student

2. Never made the honor roll in a fairly easy public high school

3. Member of several academic honor societies

4. Earned a bachelor's degree, two master's degrees, and a doctorate of philosophy in political science thereby receiving the nickname, Fourth Degree Burns. Get it?

5. First person in his graduate school class to receive a PhD, which he earned by the time he was thirty.

6. Winner of numerous teaching and service awards, including **Who's Who in Teaching**, **2003–2004**, Loyola University Faculty Senate Award for Teaching, Loyola's Black Student Union's Award for Excellence, Outstanding Young Alumni from the University of Connecticut 2001, and an Official Citation from the Connecticut General Assembly in Recognition of Service to the Students at Trinity College.

7. Author of numerous articles on urban and racial and ethnic politics.

8. Author of **Electoral Politics Is Not Enough** (2006), which examines the conditions under which white leaders identify and respond to African American and Latino interests.[9]

NOTES

1. My college baseball career lasted three days. I did not make it past the first cut. Obviously, the coach could not evaluate talent.

2. I really hope my mother does not read this book!

3. I have neither the heart nor the stomach to look at my high school transcript, so my memory will have to do.

4. Kathryn M. Doherty, "Changing Urban Education: Defining the Issues," in *Changing Urban Education*, ed. Clarence N. Stone (Lawrence: University Press of Kansas, 1998).

5. Ronit Bogler and Anit Somech, "Motives to Study and Socialization Tactics among University Students," *Journal of Social Psychology* 142, no. 2 (2002): 233–48.

6. Carolyn W. Kern, Nancy S. Fagley, and Paul Miller, "Correlates of College Retention and GPA: Learning and Study Strategies, Testwiseness, Attitudes, and ACT," *Journal of College Counseling* 1, no. 1 (1998): 26–34.

7. Trevor V. Hodge and Carlton Pickron, "Preparing Students for Success in the Academy," *Black Issues in Higher Education* 21, no. 20 (2004): 130.

8. For those who watched *Melrose Place*, I know that one of that show's main characters was Dr. Peter Burns, played by Jack Wagner. In fact, my PhD was conferred upon me on the very day that show went off the air, so Jack Wagner's last day as Dr. Peter Burns was my first day as Dr. Peter Burns. I also know that Mr. Burns is one of the main characters on *The Simpsons*. If I ever forget, some student always reminds me.

9. Peter F. Burns, *Electoral Politics Is Not Enough: Racial and Ethnic Minorities in Urban Politics* (Albany, NY: SUNY Press, 2006).

1

What Is the Goal of Your Collegiate Experience?

The Goal Is to Learn

Let me preface this chapter by stating that I was, and to a large extent still am, Mr. Grades. I used to calculate my GPA in my head during class. I believe grades are really important, but I now know that learning is the purpose of a college education. Hopefully, the more you learn, the higher your grades will be, but unfortunately this is not always the case.

You have to want to do well!

You have to want it!

A year or so ago, I sat next to a college student on a plane flight as we both returned home for Christmas vacation. I asked about her semester. She said she performed well and explained that her GPA was about a 3.5, which is excellent. Then I asked if she studied regularly, attended class, and worked hard. She said not really, but that did not matter to her because her GPA was high. I asked if her goal was to earn a high GPA. She said yes, and I disagreed. She responded with a puzzled look. I told her that learning should be her goal, which she did not achieve because she didn't work hard, attend class regularly, or complete the assigned readings. In total, she did not maximize the amount she *could* have learned.

Remember, professors cannot test students on all the lectures and readings. They lecture and assign readings so students will learn. If students do not care, they will not learn. Grades do not always reflect learning, but they are usually related. On rare occasions I received high grades with little effort in some classes, but I also worked hard for a couple of C's.

Research says, "More students believed success in a course was measured by good grades rather than by mastery of new material."[1]

THE GOLDEN RULE OF HARD WORK

How do you prepare for college? Hard work is my golden rule. I believe that hard work, and not intelligence, strongly influences learning and grades at the collegiate level. When you walk onto campus as a first-year student, you have already checked your intellectual credits at the door. The university knows you can do its work, and that is why it admitted you. I do not advise you to rely strictly on your intelligence. I have seen many students with extremely high ACT or SAT scores and nearly perfect high school GPAs who believed inaccurately that they could neglect to work hard or study and still receive good grades in college.

When you walk onto campus as a first-year student, you have already checked your intellectual credentials at the door.

You must want to do well. If you lack the desire to succeed and you do not work to accomplish this goal, then you will not make the most of the college experience. Attitude is important. You need to prepare to work hard for an entire semester, which usually runs about sixteen weeks. Hard work consists of attending all your classes, reading the assignments, and studying, even when you do not feel like it. Studying occurs any time a student does schoolwork. Forms of studying include reading books and other assigned materials, writing papers, attending on-campus lectures with other scholars, and copying notes. Studying is more than simply preparing for exams.

Studying occurs any time a student does schoolwork. Forms of studying include reading books and other assigned materials, writing papers, and copying notes. Studying is more than simply preparing for exams.

College is hard work, and you must be ready to meet this challenge. The semester rolls on with or without you, so make sure you are prepared. The advice in this book helps those who are committed to working hard. If you do not work hard, then there is no advice that can help you learn.

Determination carried me through my early years in college. No matter what grades I received, I bounced back and learned from my mistakes. In my first semester, I struggled in my Introduction to American Government course. About seventy-five students took this class, and I sat in the back of a fairly large lecture hall. I received a D or an F on the first test. It was one of the first times that I tried and failed. I was disappointed and depressed. The next day, I asked the professor how to improve. Throughout the rest of the semester, I met with the professor to discuss my progress and to gain advice on how to write better exams. The professor even showed me essays by A students, and seeing the difference between their essays and mine really helped. I pulled out a B-minus in this course, and my dedication helped me earn this grade.

You are a college student, not an employee at the excuse factory. Hard work rather than excuses should explain your performance.

At one university, I referred to some of my students as employees at the excuse factory. I used this phrase in jest, but the students understood my point. I would not accept excuses for their performance. Beware of excuses. They take the burden off you and impair your ability to improve. Each of the excuses listed in Table 1.1 takes the onus off the student and places it onto someone (usually the professor) or something (usually the subject) else. Students use these excuses as crutches to avoid hard work. If you find yourself relying on phrases such as "the professor hates me," "I do not do well in subjects outside my major," or "the professor is boring," then you may be providing yourself with excuses for not working hard. Professors do not hate students. If they did, they would not last long as professors. Students must work harder to excel in subjects outside their major, and if you want to learn, then you must work with all of your professors, even the nonengaging types. *You should reject* your *excuses for not performing well.*

Table 1.1.   Common Excuses Used by Students to Explain Poor Grades

The professor hates me.
The professor is boring.
I do not perform well on multiple-choice tests.
The professor did not realize that I take four other classes.
The exam did not accurately reflect how much I learned.
Everyone else is much smarter than I am.
I am not smart enough.
The class was too hard.
The class had too much homework.
I hate math (or some other subject).
I could write only so much with a 5,000-word limit.
The professor did not tell us what would be on the exam.
The professor is too liberal/conservative.

After reading an earlier draft of this book, one student asked, "Why do you think students make excuses?" My initial response was that excuses take the burden away from the student. It is hard to take responsibility for your mistakes because those errors say something bad about you. Certainly, I don't like to think bad things about myself. After reflecting on this question a bit further, I also believe that excuses enable students to avoid hard work. If grades are the by-products of some factor beyond one's control, then students never need to work hard. Students who regard their grades as their responsibility understand that they must study in order to succeed. They also know that their performance will suffer if they do not work hard. This is a hard but essential lesson to learn.

As my college years rolled on, my experience and dedication helped me earn even better grades. In the first semester, students lack the experience to handle college classes. Some freshmen excel without this experience, but many struggle. I survived and received a 2.9 GPA in my first semester because I studied constantly. Students who neither work hard nor possess the experience to cope with college usually end up with disastrous first semesters.

Burns's Rules for the College Experience

1. *Work hard*
2. *Stay motivated*
3. *Avoid excuses for your performance*

NOTE

1. William M. Miley and Sonia Gonsalves, "Grade Expectations: Redux," *College Student Journal* 38, no. 3 (2004): 327–32.

2

Expectations

This Isn't High School, Toto

You can prepare mentally for the college experience. The first semester is extremely important because it sets the base for your final GPA. If you get a 0.778 in semester 1, then your overall GPA will probably fail to exceed 3.0.[1] Many students never recover from a disastrous first semester. Other students who earn low GPAs initially spend the rest of their time in college trying to boost their GPA. You want to build a solid GPA from the beginning.

To prepare for the first semester, I advise you to have expectations. You need to know that if done correctly, college is hard. Many students tell me how stressed they are and how hard college is, especially at the end of the semester. I remember telling my grandfather the same thing when I attended college. Without hesitation, my grandfather asked who told me college would be easy. It is supposed to be hard, he explained. His words did little to soothe me at the time, but he was right. College is difficult, and students must deal with this reality.

College life is challenging, stressful, and difficult—but it is not impossible. In many instances, universities set the bar at a high but attainable level. University life can be overwhelming, especially in the first semester.

Learning and good grades must be your two top priorities.

You need to establish priorities. Learning and good grades must be your two top priorities. For many students, college is about partying and meeting people. Movies and the media glamorize these aspects of college life, and many students party and hook up at school. Relaxing and socializing have important places in any stage of life, but you must have balance and priorities. I think you should relax, meet others, party, and date while you are in college, but many students think that partying and fraternizing are the primary purposes of college. They emulate *Animal House* and ruin their college careers. Like Mr. Germe said, if you want to learn, then you should go to college. If you attend college only because you do not want to work or you are in search of the best time of your life, then you should save your parents' money and get a job.

Having a good time is part of college, but learning is the purpose of college.

What is your priority? You need to think long and hard about the answer to this question. In the summer of 1988, I contemplated this question and concluded that grades constituted my primary objective at UConn. Later, grades and knowledge became my tandem main concerns. I am glad I made academics my priority.

You should expect that you can more than competently complete the work assigned to you. Whereas some students have no expectations of college, others wonder whether they can perform at the university level. I was in this group. You may hear the voices of self-doubt on many occasions. Ignore those voices. You can do it.

Many students believe that high school and college are the same, or at least similar, but expectations of students are vastly different at these two levels. Generally speaking, high school teachers set rules, make assignments, and assign grades with the assumption that students are children. This assumption means that high school students face low levels of accountability and responsibility and the importance of self-discipline is limited. In college, professors assume that students are adults. With this assumption firmly in mind, professors expect high levels of accountability and responsibility from students and they emphasize self-discipline.

Several students in general, and many freshmen in particular, say to me, "I can take an 8:00 A.M. class because I got up at 6:00 A.M. in high school" or "I can handle six courses because that's how many I took in high school." These statements scare me. They indicate that students do not understand that high school and college life are dissimilar. More specifically, they suggest that students do not understand that their lives will be much different in college than they were in high school. They also reveal a misunderstanding about the differences in workload between high school and college courses.

If you make the assumption that high school and college are similar, then you will be overwhelmed by the university experience. High school and college differ in many important regards (see Table 2.1). You must recognize these differences if you are to make a relatively smooth transition to higher education. High school and college lifestyles differ to a great extent. For most of you, your parents structured your precollege life. They told you when to come home, they fed you, they made you go to bed at certain hours, and missing school on a regular basis was not an option. In college, you are in charge of your lifestyle. You decide if and when you are going to bed, which kinds of food to eat, where you want

Table 2.1.   Differences between High School and College

High School	College
Parents structure your life	You structure your life
Attendance is mandatory	Attendance is voluntary
Intelligence leads to good grades and respect	Intelligence is a given
Subjects covered in a month or two	Subjects covered in a week or two

to sleep, if and when you want to wake up, and whether you want to attend class. Many students cannot handle this responsibility.

In my opinion, many students fail or do not excel in their first semester because they did not get themselves to class, they did not study, and they lacked self-discipline. As I said earlier, time and dedication, rather than intelligence, affect success in college, especially in the early years. Even the most gifted students cannot excel if they do not show up to class, take tests, or turn in assignments.

Others say, "Students graduate high school under one set of coursework standards only to discover that three months later, they must meet a whole new set of standards in college. Students are simply not getting the information they need about what it takes to succeed in higher education."[2]

High school and college courses differ. The content in college courses is more detailed than that presented in high school. You will handle more material in a shorter period of time in college than you did in high school. College reading is more intense and, in many instances, more dense. Subjects you learned in weeks in high school may be covered in days in college.

Research says, "Asked to evaluate their own level of preparation on six separate dimensions [oral communication/public speaking, science, mathematics, doing research, quality of writing that is expected, and reading/understanding complicated materials], only 14% of college students feel that they are generally able to do what is expected of them in all dimensions."[3]

Many college professors will not check your progress, and, as one former student explained, "whether or not you succeed does not matter to them." If you do not show up, they will not care. If you do not hand in assignments, they will not care. If you have a failing grade at the midterm, professors will not contact your parents. Professors have no problem assigning F's to you. You determine your success in college. As

I explain in chapter 9, many professors will work with you as long as you exhibit the desire and drive to warrant that partnership. If you cut corners, then your professors will not help you. Your professors expect a great deal from you. They may challenge you in ways that you have not been pushed in the past.

"I don't fail students; students fail themselves."
—Dr. Matthew O. Thomas, Cal State University, Chico

College assignments differ from those in high school. In college, I assign seven-to-ten-page papers to freshmen, who have about three weeks to complete these assignments. I read rough drafts but many professors do not. Many students have no experience writing these kinds of papers. Even students who wrote longer papers before college have more freedom in college than they did in high school. By that I mean that high school teachers may require students to complete rough drafts and they may help create the paper. In college, some professors assist you in the process but many simply ask that you turn in the paper on the due date. In high school, teachers monitor students' preparation. In college, many professors know you have not prepared in advance only by the quality of your paper. A vast majority of the papers written the night before the due date are terrible.

Research says, "College instructors estimate that 42% of high school graduates are not adequately prepared by their high school education for the expectations of college classes and are struggling or having to take remedial courses to catch up."[4]

My high school tests differed from those I took in college. My high school teachers provided more clues about the content of tests than my college professors did. In high school, lectures provided the basis for tests. In college, many professors give exams based strictly on the readings. One professor told the class that we did not have to attend class because she based the exam on the readings. I had no idea how to study for a test based solely on the readings.

College professors demand more comprehensive answers than high school teachers do.

Professors use a variety of exams (for more on exams, see chapter 6). The most common exams in the humanities and social sciences are multiple choice, essays, and short answers. Math professors ask students to solve problems, whereas biology and chemistry professors use a variety of testing strategies, including quizzes and exams that include multiple-choice responses, short answers, matching, problems to solve, and fill-in-the-blanks.[5] Furthermore, papers in general, and research papers in particular, were special assignments in high school whereas they are common in college.

I lay out some of the major differences between high school and college here because students should not think of college as simply a continuation of high school. College is a unique experience with new challenges. Many students tell me they can take calculus, biology, and English in their first semester because they completed these subjects in high school. I get nervous when I hear this claim. Because courses, homework, tests, and student life are new experiences, college freshmen must make a sensible first schedule to ease their transition (see chapter 10 for more on your first schedule).

Burns's Rules for College Expectations

1. Establish priorities
2. Make academics and learning your top priorities
3. Do not believe college is simply an extension of high school

NOTES

1. The original draft of this book included 0.7 and not 0.778. When the person to whom I was referring in this sentence read this draft, he corrected me; his first-semester GPA was 0.778 and not 0.7.

2. Michael W. Kirst, "The High School/College Disconnect," *Educational Leadership* 62, no. 3 (2004): 51–55.

3. Peter D. Hart Research Associates/Public Opinion Strategies. *Rising to the Challenge: Are High School Graduates Prepared for College and Work? A Study of Recent High School Graduates, College Instructors, and Employers* (study conducted for Achieve, Inc., February 2005), available online at www.achieve.org/dstore.nsf/Lookup/pollreport/$file/pollreport.pdf, p. 4.

4. Peter D. Hart Research Associates/Public Opinion Strategies, *Rising to the Challenge.*

5. For this information, I am indebted to Stephen M. Scariano, Rosalie Anderson, and Kurt Birdwhistell.

Preparing for the Semester

How to Outrun the Avalanche

Imagine you are on the side of a snow-covered mountain in the dead of winter. Suddenly, you hear an unpleasant sound and you notice that the top of the mountain is moving. An avalanche has commenced, and you must outrun it. If you can, then you will make it to safety. The avalanche controls your moves once it catches you. Do you remember seeing cartoon characters that get caught in an avalanche and can no longer control their movements? All you see is arms and legs. The reality is that the avalanche overwhelms, tramples, and controls you. Avalanches hurt and kill.

Semesters are like avalanches. You need to outrun both. Would you wait to outrun an avalanche? Like avalanches, semesters move rapidly, and so should you.

The semester is similar to an avalanche. Semesters will not kill you and they are not about life and death. You should never worry so much about school that you become ill. No professors, however evil they appear to be, would want you to get sick over their class.[1]

Semesters are similar to avalanches because you must prepare to outrun both. You should approach the semester much the same way you would an avalanche. The avalanche commences on the *very first* day of class and ends after your last exam. If you prepare adequately and work hard, then you can thrive during the semester. If you do not prepare, the semester will overwhelm and trample you.

Semesters move rapidly and so should you. In my first semester as a student, I did not realize an avalanche had started. At the end of the first week, I started to read my assignments, and I noticed I was already behind! I needed to read about a hundred pages in a week's time to catch up. The student who rarely brought his books home and read only one book cover to cover in high school needed to read one hundred dense pages. I started to panic, and at that moment I learned the importance of starting early.

At the start of the semester, many students do nothing beyond attending class. Others start the semester not knowing which classes they should take. They did not register on time during the previous semester and they hunt for classes at the beginning of the semester. These students fall behind because they did not enroll in some of their courses until after the first full week of classes.

Professor Fettweis[2] says, "*Do not* skip a week of any classes—attend *all*. Important information and the all-important course overview are given on day 1."

Some students wait to buy their books until the week of the exam. They do not want to be part of the rush. My suggestion is to come to campus a few days early and purchase your books. The bookstore returns books about six to eight weeks into the semester. Many students go to the bookstore the week of or even the day before the exam and find that the book is either sold out or has been returned to the publisher. To avoid these headaches, I suggest that you purchase all your books before the semester begins.

"Students course shop during the first week of school. Attend all potential courses until you make your final decisions. Too many students fall behind because they stop attending classes they ultimately take."
                —Dr. Matthew O. Thomas, Cal State University, Chico

Students who do not study until the week of the exam are behind, and they remain that way throughout the semester. Students who do no work early in the semester must put all of their focus on their first test. As an example, let us say that a student waits to study until his first test, which is in calculus. This student usually spends about three days, which is entirely too little, cramming for the exam in calculus. By the time the test in calculus ends, he has fallen behind on his assignments and exams in history, French, psychology, and biology. The semester rules this student's actions. You need to control your semester.

THE SEMESTER STARTS ON DAY 1
Breaks between semesters typically last between one and three months. The university provides such a long break so students can relax and recharge. You do not want to extend this break into the semester. You should begin to study on the first day of the semester. Would you wait to outrun an avalanche?

Burns says, "The semester begins on day 1, and so should you."

Former student replies, "You cannot expect students to start studying on day 1."

Burns says, "Yes, I can. Learning and getting high grades in college are matters of will."

After panicking over the number of pages I needed to read to catch up in my first semester, I promised myself I would never experience that feeling again. Consequently, I started to read on the first night of each subsequent semester. One of my friends, who saw me reading in the lounge on the first day of the semester, said I was unbelievable. She wanted me to relax and ease into the semester. I explained that I relaxed during the summer and that the semester would not be easy with me, so I could not be easy with it. If you take a week off at the beginning of the semester, then you will be one week behind. Remember, what are your priorities? Are your priorities to catch up with your friends and go out? There is nothing wrong with renewing your friendships, but this act cannot take precedence over studying. The break is over on day 1 and you need to start reading and preparing on day 1!

If you take a week off at the beginning of the semester, you will be one week behind.

PLAN YOUR SEMESTER

Outrunning the avalanche takes planning. You should never be surprised by due dates during the semester. I see too many students come into my office on a Monday and express surprise that they have two tests and a paper due that week. Clearly, the avalanche trapped them.

You need to use your syllabi to avoid being avalanched. Professors hand out syllabi on the first day of class, or at least by the end of the first week. The syllabus summarizes the course and, in most cases, provides due dates and examination dates. If your professor does not provide these dates to you, ask him or her to let you know about due dates in advance. If the professor still refuses, then inform the department chair that the professor will not let you let you know when your assignments are due.

Others say, "The syllabus is a contract, a permanent record, and a learning tool."[3]

I never saw a syllabus until my first day of class in college. I think I had heard of a syllabus, but I did not really know what it was. Some syllabi provide more detail than others, but most include contact information, policy statements about grading and expectations, due dates, and point allocation. The title of the course and the professor's name, phone number, e-mail address, office location, and office hours usually appear on the top of the syllabus (see Figure 3.1). Make sure to attend the correct section of your course. At Loyola, the political science department offers two sections of Introduction to American Government in the fall. The top of the syllabus lets students know if they are in the right section of a course.

It is your right and even your duty to contact your professors. You can use office hours and e-mail to ask questions. If necessary, you can phone your professor, but as a professor I prefer e-mails, which I can return at my convenience. By contrast, I may be doing something when the phone rings.

The one warning I can give students regarding contacting professors is to not overdo it. College promotes independence, so please use discretion when you contact your professors (for more on professor-student relations, see chapter 9). Some students contact me on a weekly if not daily basis, and this is too much interaction. For example, one student literally knocks on my door four days a week. Clearly, this level of contact is too much. I think that visiting office hours once a month during the semester is about right. You should have a reason to visit office hours. Valid reasons include clarification of the notes, a progress report on your performance, or a discussion of the readings.

The night before the exam is an inappropriate time to contact your professors. Recently, I was working in my office at 7 P.M. and students called to ask about their exam, which was the next day. They said the readings confused them, and their questions indicated that they had waited until the night before the exam to read. If you have questions about the exam, make sure to work far

FIGURE 3.1.
A Sample Long Syllabus

[Title of course] INTRODUCTION TO AMERICAN GOVERNMENT
[Official title with section number] POLITICAL SCIENCE A100-002
Fall 2004

[Information about the professor]
Professor Smith
Office: Social Science Building 471A
Office Hours: Tuesday and Thursday 9:30 to 10:30 and by appointment
Phone: 481-3732
smith@college.edu

Students with disabilities who wish to receive accommodations in this class should contact Disability Services at 504-865-2990 as soon as possible so that warranted accommodations can be implemented in a timely fashion. Disability Services is located in the Academic Enrichment Center.

[Professor's goals]
I. Goals:

The goal of this class is to learn.

During this course we will learn more about not only American government but also how to read, write, and think more critically.

Political Science A100-002 introduces you to the basic concepts of American government and politics. This course is designed to increase your knowledge of the following areas: the theoretical underpinnings of this government, the operation of American institutions and politics, and the roles citizens play in American governmental processes. It is also designed to improve your analytical, critical writing, critical thinking, and communications skills. Remember that your ability to develop and perform these skills is as important to you as the information that you will take from this course.

The themes of majority rule and minority rights, separation of powers, checks and balances, federalism, and power in representation are prevalent throughout this course. In each of the following parts and in each class, we will ask ourselves how these concepts affect American politics. Keep these themes in mind throughout the course and focus upon them in your readings, writings, and dialogue.

Throughout the course, you need to understand the concepts of independent and dependent variables. The actions of independent variables affect the dependent variable. For example, if opening an umbrella is your dependent variable, then rain is one independent variable. That is, the action of opening the umbrella depends partly upon whether it is raining. In this course, for example, we need to consider the effect of the Articles of Confederation on the new Constitution.

In this course, we will also analyze how scholars make knowledge claims. That is, how do researchers and students support their assertions? How do they know what they claim?

[Different parts of the course]
II. Parts:

The course is divided into three parts: foundations of government, institutions of government, and people and politics.

Part one investigates the theoretical foundations of American government. This section emphasizes American political thought and ideology; it concentrates on the concepts that drove the Founding Fathers, and it focuses on the liberties, rights, and privileges that every American should possess.

Part two examines the institutions of American government. We study the executive, legislative, and judicial branches separately but we must always keep in mind how these institutions interact with each other. Questions that guide this section include which branch of government did the Framers think would be most powerful? Which branch of government is the most powerful today? How does each of these branches gain power by representing powerful groups and constituencies? In this section we will also analyze the effect that the bureaucracy—the silent branch—exerts on the workings of American institutions and policies.

The final part explores the people and politics of American government. We will look at how public opinion, the mass media, and interest groups influence majority rule and minority rights, federalism, separation of powers, checks and balances, and power in representation. We will also examine how political parties, voting and elections, and the campaign process affect policymakers, politics, and policies.

(continued)

FIGURE 3.1.
Continued

Part One: Foundations of Government
a. Ideology
b. The Constitution
c. Federalism
d. Civil Liberties
e. Civil Rights
Part Two: Institutions of Government/Policymakers
a. Congress
b. The Presidency
c. The Judiciary
d. The Bureaucracy
Part Three: People and Politics
a. Public Opinion
b. Political Parties
c. Voting and Elections
d. The Campaign Process
e. Mass Media
f. Interest Groups

[Professor's expectations of students]
III. Expectations:
    a. You should attend every class. I will not deduct points from your grade for class absences, but missing class will certainly affect your ability to learn and it will almost certainly affect your grade in a negative way. By contrast, attending all classes will enhance your learning experience and almost certainly improve your grade.
    b. You will lose points from your final grade if you are late to class on a regular basis.
    c. You are responsible for reading the entire assignment before class. If you are assigned chapter 1 for the first class, please have the entire chapter read before that class.
    d. This class will consist of lectures and class discussion but there will tend to be more of the former than the latter. Let me assure you that this course is designed for you. If you have any questions about the material please feel free to ask me immediately.

[What students can expect from the professor of this course]
IV. Expectations of Professor:

a. While I expect you to work hard and to prepare on a daily basis, let me assure you that I will be there to help you. Please come and see me in my office hours or by appointment. Even if you are not having any difficulty with the material, please come and see me. My door is always open.

b. American government is such an interesting subject. You should expect to enjoy this learning experience as long as you read the material before class, attend class, prepare constantly, and work hard. If you perform these tasks, then you will do very well in this course.

[How the professor will calculate your grade]
[Assignments and point values of assignments also listed]
V. Grading:

Your grade consists of the following:

1. Three in-class examinations constitute 75 percent of your grade. You need to provide me with a blue book at least one class before each exam. Please write your name on the blue book, which you can purchase at the bookstore.

   The first in-class examination covers the readings and lectures from Weeks 1 through 4. The second exam covers readings and lectures from Weeks 5 through 13. The noncumulative final covers the rest of the semester.

   The exams will probably include some combination of identifications, short essays, longer essays, and open-ended questions. For the identifications, which come from the book and the lectures, you need to not only define the term but also relate it to the themes of the course. That is, why is this term significant? So what?

   The detailed essay asks you to write on a major subject. I might provide the essay question to you in advance. If so, then you can use a one-page outline that I approve.

   A-quality identification and essay answers contain great insight. They indicate that you have reflected on the topic. A answers include the who, what, where, and when questions, but they also explore the why and how questions and what the readings say about American government. A answers contain proper grammar, do not include any spelling or factual mistakes, and illustrate you have completed and reflected upon the readings.

   (continued)

FIGURE 3.1.
Continued

B- and C-quality tests get all or most of the facts correct but do not indicate that the student has thought long and hard about the assignment. B and C exams answer the who, what, where, and when questions but they neither reflect upon the why and how questions nor explain what the readings say about American government.

D and F answers are incomplete, include spelling and grammar mistakes, contain many incorrect assertions, and are not quality work. They do not adequately answer the who, what, were, when, why, or how questions.

Examinations = 75 percent
[Due dates]
Exam Schedule:
Examination One is Thursday, September 23
Examination Two is Tuesday, October 26
Examination Three is December 14 at 9:00 a.m.

2. A short paper makes up the other 25 percent of your grade.

The topic asks you to determine which branch of government has the most power and why.

While this question asks for your opinion, you must support your opinion with facts. You must discuss why the branch that you selected is more powerful than the other two. This requires that you discuss (and compare) all three branches of government.

You must support your answer with information from the readings and the class. Do not base your answers on outside information. This is not to say that you cannot use outside sources. However, base your answers on the readings, the class, and the homework assignments.

Remember that you must support your answer with facts.

The following are guidelines that you must follow in answering your paper.

1. Provide a thesis type statement that lets the reader know what you are proving.

2. Consider the various components of the question before you start writing so that you base your answer on information drawn from careful consideration of the class and the readings.

The paper must be typewritten and double-spaced with margins that are at least 1" all around. The font must be 12 point.

Points will be deducted if these requirements are not met. The paper can be no longer than seven (7) pages.

Please see the suggestions for writing a better paper on my website (http://www.loyno.edu/~pburns/). You must also use either MLA Citation Style or *The Chicago Manual of Style* to cite your sources. Points will be deducted if you do not follow the writing tips and the style requirements. You will lose two points for each spelling mistake and each grammar mistake.

[Another due date]
This paper is due in class December 2
Short paper = 25 percent

[More on grading. These are the details to which you should pay attention.]
VI. Grading Policies:

If any paper is late, you will lose one full letter grade. In addition, you will lose one full letter grade for each additional day the paper is late.

For each assignment, unless we make special arrangements, late papers include those you slip under my door while class is taking place, e-mailed assignments, or assignments that you hand in at the end of a class that you did not attend. Please do not e-mail your paper to me unless we make special arrangements. I am very flexible, which means that I will make special arrangements with you when extraordinary circumstances arise and you cannot hand in the assignment on time. Please make sure that all written assignments are top-quality work, which means that you write in complete ideas and in complete sentences.

You, and only you, must write and complete each assignment. Each assignment should reflect your ideas and your writing. You cannot consult with others unless they are library staff or other professors. Papers cannot be team-written. You must work independently. Do not discuss the paper or get assistance from others unless they are library staff or other professors. If you want to interview someone for your project, please consult with me. I will read drafts of your paper but only up to one week before the paper is due. I will be happy to discuss your paper with you at any time, but your paper will improve if we meet earlier rather than later.

(continued)

FIGURE 3.1.
Continued

[What constitutes an A through F]
[Some schools offer minuses and pluses and others do not. At this school, pluses but not minuses are awarded.]

VII. Grading Scale:

    90−100 = A
    87−89 = B+
    80−86 = B
    77−79 = C+
    70−76 = C
    67−69 = D+
    60−66 = D
     0−59 = F

[Other various rules. Attention to detail is key here. Many students do not read this section.]

VIII. Other Points of Interest :

Please avoid sidebar conversations during class. If you talk while another student or the professor is addressing the class, then I will deduct points from your final grade.

Please be respectful of the other students and the professor in this course. Disruptive behavior will not be tolerated and will result in a lower grade and other penalties.

Please do not get up during class unless it is an emergency. You will lose points if you continually get up during class.

[How to receive extra credit. Many students do not read this section.]

If I give you extra-credit assignments during the class, then you must follow these guidelines to receive credit.

a. You must be in attendance when I assign the extra-credit opportunity. You will not be eligible for the extra-credit opportunity if you received an excused absence.

b. If applicable, you must answer the extra-credit assignment.

c. If applicable, you must type the extra-credit assignment.

d. If applicable, you must turn in the paper one week after I assign the topic.

e. Unless otherwise instructed, the extra-credit assignment should be no longer than one page.

f. The values of the extra-credit assignments may vary.

g. The maximum number of extra-credit points you can add to your final grade is two.

[Readings for the course. You should bring that day's reading to class.]
IX. Required Texts: (Please bring books to class)
1. Edwards, George C. III, Martin P. Wattenberg, and Robert L. Lineberry. 2001. *Government in America: People, Politics, and Policy* (11th ed.). New York: Longman.
2. Please check my website on a regular basis. The site will have important information about the class.
3. The other readings will be available on reserve in the library.
4. Please bring that day's reading material to class.

[Dates the professor will cover the material.]
X. Assignments:
                                Week
  I. August 31–September 2
    ▪ Introduction and Overview
  II. September 7–9
    ▪ Read Chapter 1—Introducing Government in America
    ▪ Overview of major themes, including majority rule and minority rights, checks and balances and separation of powers, federalism, and power in representation.
  III. September 14–16
    ▪ Read Chapter 2—The Constitution
    ▪ Read Federalist Papers 15 and 51
    ▪ See http://www.law.ou.edu/hist/federalist/ for a copy of the Federalist Papers
    ▪ Read the Constitution
    ▪ Read de Tocqueville's "Origins and Democratic Social Conditions of Anglo-Americans"
  IV. September 21
    ▪ More on the Constitution
    ▪ Read Hofstadter's "The Founding Fathers: An Age of Realism"
  V. September 23
    ▪ Exam #1 on all lectures and readings to this point
  VI. September 28–30
    ▪ Federalism
    ▪ Read Chapter 3—Federalism
    ▪ Read Federalist 46
    ▪ Read David Walker's "Two Hundred Years of American Federalism"
    ▪ Read John Marshall from *McCulloch v. Maryland*

(*continued*)

FIGURE 3.1.
Continued

VII. October 5–7
- Continuation of Federalism and Start of Civil Liberties—Read Chapter 4—Civil Liberties
- Read Harry Blackmun from *Roe v. Wade*
- Read *Gitlow v. New York*
- Read *Mapp v. Ohio*
- Read *Miranda v. Arizona*

VIII. October 12–14
- Read Chapter 5—Civil Rights and Public Policy
- Read Hugo L. Black from *Korematsu v. United States*

IX. October 19
- Fall Break Holiday—No Class

X. October 21
- Read Chapter 12—Congress
- Read Richard Fenno's "Home Style"
- Read Paul Starobin's "Pork: A Time-Honored Tradition Lives On"
- Read Woodrow Wilson's "Congressional Government"

XI. October 26
- Exam #2 on all lectures and readings from Exam #1 to this point

XII. October 28
- Congress continued and start of the Presidency—Read Chapter 13
- Read David R. Mayhew's "Congress: The Electoral Connection"
- Read Roger H. Davidson and Walter J. Oleszek's "Congress and Its Members"
- Read Richard Neustadt's "The Power to Persuade"

XIII. November 2–4

XIV. November 9–11
- Read Chapter 16—The Federal Courts
- Read Federalist 78
- Read David O'Brien's "The Court and American Life"
- Read John Marshall from *Marbury v. Madison*
- Read Martin M. Shapiro's "The Presidency and the Federal Courts"

XV. November 16–18
- Read Chapter 15—The Federal Bureaucracy
- Read James Q. Wilson's "Bureaucracy: What Government Agencies Do and Why They Do It"

XVI. November 23
- Read Chapter 6—Public Opinion and Political Action (From "How Americans Learn about Politics: Political Socialization" to (but not including) "Understanding Public Opinion and Political Action")
- Read Chapter 7—Mass Media and the Political Agenda (From "The News and Public Opinion" to the end of the chapter)
- Read George Gallup's "Polling the Public"
- Read V. O. Key's "Public Opinion and American Democracy"

XVII. November 25
- No Class—Thanksgiving

XVIIII. November 30
- Read Chapter 8—Political Parties
- Read Chapter 10—Elections and Voting Behavior (From "Whether to Vote: A Citizen's First Choice" to the end of the chapter)
- Read Chapter 9—Nominations and Campaigns (From "The Campaign Game" to the end of the chapter); Read Morris P. Fiorina's "The Decline of Collective Responsibility in American Politics"
- Read Walter Dean Burnham's "The Turnout Problem"

XIX. December 2
- Read Chapter 11—Interest Groups (entire)
- Read Federalist 10
- Read Mancur Olson's "Collective Action: The Logic"

XX. December 7–9
XXI. December 14 (9 a.m.–11 a.m.) Final Exam

enough in advance in order to ask questions during office hours. In this scenario, these students abused my collegial nature.

You should only call a professor's home if you are given permission by the instructor. Some instructors provide their home numbers to students because they work at home. I would call only at reasonable hours (after 10 A.M. before 8 P.M.), and I would not phone the night before the exam.

Many professors include statements about their policies, expectations, grading procedures, and due dates on their syllabi. Students must know and understand these sections. As I explain in chapter 9, professors attempt to instill values in students, and they award points for these values. For instance, professors who attach importance to attendance and participation will allocate percentage points toward your final grade based upon how often you come to class and speak during the semester. The expectations and goals provide insight into the subjects, topics, and themes of greatest importance to the professor.

In the expectations section of the American Government syllabus, I inform students that I value regular attendance, promptness, and reading the entire assignment before the class (see my longer American Government syllabus). The syllabus also lets students know that I will assist them in the learning process if they seek my help.

The grading procedures section allows students to know whether exams, papers, discussion, or assignments form the basis of the grade. It also provides the point allocation for each assignment. At the end of most semesters, students e-mail me and ask, "How did I get this grade?" They ask this question because they never read the point allocation section of the syllabus.

For my American Government course, three exams and a paper make up the student's grade. The syllabus spells out the contents of each exam and the essay topic. It also provides the dates upon which the students will take the exams and hand in their papers.

The syllabus lays out my standards for A's, B's, C's, and below. It also informs students about what I regard as late papers. This information is vital for students to earn high grades, but for the most part only the best students consult the syllabus on a regular basis.

Due dates inform students about when they will be expected take exams or hand in papers. Many syllabi also specify the dates upon which various subjects will be covered. In my American Government syllabus, I include the topics I will address each week. I want to let the students know when I will cover certain areas. In weeks three and four of my course, for instance, the lectures and readings cover the Constitution. In other more general syllabi, professors include the topics they will cover but they do not specify the dates upon which these subjects will be studied (see Figure 3.2).

Once you receive all your syllabi, make a master calendar denoting all due dates and exam days. I would mark each class in a different color. You should prepare a game plan once you have marked all your assignment dates, including the final exam dates. Here are a few ways to formulate a game plan for the semester. First, compare your classes and look for the course(s) with heavy reading loads and numerous assignments. These courses require extra attention. Second, look for the earliest assignments. Some professors assign quizzes or short papers in the second week of the semester. You need to start preparing immediately for these assignments. Next, look for megaprojects, which require extra time. Do you have a major term paper due in six weeks? Whereas six weeks seems like an eternity, it is not. As the semester rolls on, you grow more tired, you take on more social and academic responsibilities, and suddenly the sixth week of the semester arrives. Assignments should never surprise you. Fourth, plan around your social activities. If friends visit on a particular weekend, then you need to work ahead so as to not fall behind. Most universities hold

FIGURE 3.2.
A Sample Short Syllabus[4]

[Title of Course] American Government
Political Science 101-01 [Official title with section number]
Spring 2005

[Information about the professor]
Dr. Jones
Social Science Bldg. Room 808
865-2121
[Professor's goals]

This course provides an overview of the structure, development, and powers of the national government. Special attention is paid to the Constitutional Convention and the effects of its deliberations on the United States today.

[Different parts of the course]

Topics to be Covered	Chapters
The Beginning	1 and 2
Federalism	3
The Presidency	6, 9, 10, and 11
The Congress	5
The Judiciary	7 and 4

[Due dates]

The first test is scheduled for Friday, February 11, and it will cover the lectures to date. Lowi and Ginsberg's *American Government* is the textbook recommended, but it is not required. The tests will come only from the lectures.

The second test is scheduled for Wednesday, March 16, and it will cover the lectures between the first and second test.

The third test will be held on Wednesday, May 4, and it will cover the lectures from the second exam until the end of the course. *There is no final exam.*

Class Policies
Office: Social Science Building Room 471—Tuesday/Thursday 9:30-11
A.M., and by appointment.

The grading scale in this course is as follows: 0–59 = F; 60-64 = D;
65–69 = D+; 70–74 = C; 75–79 = C+; 80–84 = B; 85–89 = B+; 90–94
= A; 95–100 = A+. *Each test counts for one-third of the final grade.* [How
the professor will calculate your grade]

[Various rules. Attention to detail is key here. Many students do not read
this section.]

Anyone having absences of more than 15 percent of the semester's
classes is subject to an F grade for the course. Any absence should be excused prior to the test. Late arrival for class counts as an absence if roll
has been taken.

A student may withdraw from the class with a W up to and including Friday, April 1.

It is recommended that no notes, paper, or books be brought to class on
test days. *If anything is* brought by a student except a pen, *it must be*
placed in an area designated by the professor. Paper will be provided by
the professor. No other paper may be used on test days. *Any cheating on
a test will result in an F grade for the course.*

If any changes are made in the test schedule or material to be covered in
the test, at least one week's notice will be given in class. If the university
cancels classes on a day an exam is scheduled, the exam will be given on
the next scheduled class day the university is in session.

spring weekends with bands and parties. You want to take part
in these activities, but not at the expense of falling behind. As
you plan your semester, you should account for these social activities and work ahead. You will thank yourself if you plan
ahead.

Your assignments should never surprise you.

Avalanches are cumulative. As they progress, they collect
more snow and more strength. In a similar sense, semesters are

cumulative. Professors tend to schedule exams and assignments at the same points of the semester. The days before a vacation are prime targets for exams. Professors like to spend extra time grading exams on their off days. Furthermore, some universities tell professors when midterm grades are due or when they should give midterm exams. Sure enough, most professors schedule their exams for that week. Consequently, your assignments are cumulative. All your course examinations may take place on the same day during the semester. If you do not know this is the case, then you cannot prepare in advance. If you cannot prepare in advance, the avalanche of the semester will overtake you and you will not learn.

What do I mean by work in advance? Many of my advisees and students tell me they worked hard on a particular assignment or exam. When I ask how long they spent on this assignment, the answer is frequently two or three days. Two to three days is not enough to time to prepare for a college-level examination or paper. I believe that time strongly affects grades. Grades and learning improve when students dedicate time and energy to their studies.

Two or three days are not enough time to prepare for a college-level examination or paper. The amount of time a student prepares for a test or paper strongly affects grades and learning.

IMPORTANCE OF PLANNING AHEAD

If you map out your semester, you can prepare weeks in advance for tests and exams. Students could not believe me the first time I told them to work weeks in advance. I worked weeks in advance, I have seen other students work weeks in advance, and you can work weeks in advance as well. You can only work weeks ahead of your assignments if you start on day 1.

Research says, "Results from the latest National Survey of Student Engagement . . . found that only 12 percent of last year's freshmen at four-year residential colleges reported spending 26 or more hours per week preparing for classes, while the majority, 63 percent, said they spend 15 or fewer hours on class preparation, which the survey defines as 'studying, reading, writing, rehearsing, and other activities related to your academic program.'"[5]

To convince students to work ahead, I tell them about a person chopping down a large tree. What is the most efficient and effective way to chop down a tree? I submit that the best way to chop a tree down is to work at it a little at a time. If you work at the tree for one hour a day, then your blows are sharp and you have maximum strength. After one hour, you lose strength and concentration and it takes longer to achieve what you did in the first hour. Each day when you return to the tree, you have thought about your effort, and you have a new perspective that may help you.

Others say, "The most commonly prescribed amount [of study time] is at least two hours of class preparation for every hour spent in the classroom—meaning 25 to 30 hours a week for a typical full-time student. The idea is that students should consider college their full-time job, and that class time and preparation should take about 40 hours each week. That's long been the conventional wisdom."[6]

I often tell students my jigsaw puzzle story to illustrate my point about the effect preparation exerts on perspective and performance. When I was a senior in college, my friends, my family, and I worked on this giant jigsaw puzzle during a snowstorm. After focusing on the puzzle for hours, my father said, "That's it, I am going sled riding, and then I will finish the puzzle." Ha! I thought. I will show him. I will stay here and finish the puzzle while he and my friends play. Suffice it to say, I could not find any pieces, and they finished the puzzle when they returned. I had no perspective as I sat there for hours. They had a fresh perspective after playing outside. Students who pull all-nighters and work on a paper for a few days have a narrow perspective on their papers. They do not have the benefit of putting it away, returning, cutting the unclear material, copyediting, and polishing. Students who prepare in advance have a fresh perspective, and their often papers reflect this point of view.

Professor Fettweis says, "I've told students to approach school like it was their job."

If you begin working weeks in advance, then you are fresh each time you write or prepare. Under this scenario, you exert maximum energy and concentration. Furthermore, each day when you return to your assignment or notes, you see aspects you missed. Students who work in advance tend to have fewer proofreading mistakes than those who do not.

In most instances, the avalanche topples the unprepared person. Under certain circumstances, however, the avalanche buries those who carry too much. You should be careful not to bite off more than you can chew, especially in your first semester. When students arrive at college, they often experience sensory overload. Universities and colleges offer a variety of activities, including fraternities and sororities, intramural sports, clubs, parties, sporting events, and the theater, to name a few. You should try many of these activities, but not necessarily in one semester in general, or in your first semester in particular. Many hardworking students get avalanched because they carry too many responsibilities. Student government, clubs, and service constitute important parts of the college experience, but they should not take precedence over your studies. When in doubt, return to the question you answered before you began your college career—why are you attending college in the first place? I understand that some students must work and that unemployment is often not an option, but many students can choose to space out their activities. It is important to concentrate on academics first and then add other activities as your college career progresses.

Burns's Rules for How to Prepare for the Semester

1. Start your schoolwork as soon as the semester begins
2. Plan your semester's academic and extracurricular activities at the beginning of the semester
3. Know your syllabi
4. Consult syllabi on a regular basis
5. Prepare in advance for your studies

NOTES

1. For this information I am indebted to Patty Burns.

2. Christopher J. Fettweis, a graduate-school colleague and close friend, read drafts of the book. Chris, aka the Captain and the Team, holds a PhD from the University of Maryland, is the author of several journal articles on international security, and teaches at the Naval War College. He offered some great insight, which I included throughout the book.

3. Jay Parkes and Mary B. Harris, "The Purposes of a Syllabus," *College Teaching* 50, no. 2 (2002): 55–61.

4. This is a slightly modified version of a colleague's syllabus.

5. Jeffrey R. Young, "Homework? What Homework?" *Chronicle of Higher Education* 49, no. 15 (2002), available online at chronicle.com/free/v49/i15/15a03501.htm.

6. Young, "Homework? What Homework?"

4

Stages of the Semester
Will You Work Hard during the Dog Days?

Semesters come in stages and some individuals perform their best during certain parts of the semester (see Table 4.1). Mike Vacca, my high school baseball coach, emphasized consistency throughout the season. He never wanted the team to get too high after a win or too low after a loss. I think you should approach the semester and all its stages in much the same way. You will notice others who appear to outwork you during one stage. My advice is to ignore them. You need consistency in your effort. Here is how I conceive of the different phases of the semester and the different actors within each.

SPRINTERS (WEEKS 1 TO 2 OF THE SEMESTER)
As the label implies, sprinters begin the marathon-like semester by vigorously approaching their schoolwork. Their spirit is strong at the beginning of the semester, but they run out of gas by about the third week. You must create regular and sensible study habits (for more on study habits, see chapter 5). You probably cannot keep up a furious pace for sixteen weeks. The sprinters fade over time.

The sprinters resemble people who make New Year's resolutions to exercise and lose weight. Both start with great intensity, but they create unrealistic expectations that they cannot meet. Just as people can-

Table 4.1.   Tour de Semester

Stage	Time	Winner of the Stage	Outcome
1. Sprinter	Weeks 1 to 2	Usually a student on academic probation or one who came off a poor semester	Sprinters fade and tend to neither learn nor receive good grades
2. Dog Days of the Semester	Weeks 3 to 14	Hard workers; dedicated students	Winners of this stage tend to learn and receive good grades
3. Library Campers	Weeks 15 to 16	Students who neither worked hard nor prepared on a consistent basis during the first 14 weeks of the semester	No substantial changes to semester GPA

not quickly go from not exercising to running the New York City Marathon, students cannot quickly transform from barely studying to preparing all day and night. A more reasonable expectation is to study for short spurts each day and to plan to keep that schedule for the entire semester.

THE LIBRARY CAMPERS (WEEKS 15 TO 16)

So-called library campers overtake the library in the final two weeks of the semester. I have noticed them at each college/university with which I have been associated. As the label suggests, these students set up a camp in the library for the final two weeks of the semester. They bring all their books and notes into the library and overtake a carrel or even a section of the library. They often carry around thirty-two-ounce coffee mugs. For the most part, library campers are delusional. They believe they can save a semester by studying for two weeks straight. At the conclusion of this two-week period, they leave the library with a false sense of accomplishment. You should not believe that you can make up a semester's worth of work in two weeks.

DOG DAYS OF THE SEMESTER (WEEKS 3 TO 14)

Learning occurs and grades form during the dog days of the semester. These are the times in which the sprinters fade and the library campers have yet to show up. During the dog days, you can see neither the beginning nor the end of the semester. During these days, you need to work hard and be consistent. Anyone can attend class when they feel like it. Anyone can attend class when they believe they may fail otherwise. The special person attends every class. Attendance is always mandatory, regardless of what the syllabus says. Serious learning occurs in class and you want to be there. I knew I was achieving my goals when I attended classes that less than half of the students made. On more than one occasion I walked across a cold practice football field on the frozen tundra of Storrs, Connecticut, to attend an 8 A.M. class. The ringing of the alarm clock signals the moment of truth. Will you get up and face the elements? What if it is sleep weather, as my mother calls it? You know, sleep weather occurs when it is rainy, gray, and cold, and your bed is warm and dry. Will you get up? Those who attend classes and study on these days are winning the dog days, and their learning experience and grades will be their rewards.

Will you attend class during times of sleep weather, when it is rainy, gray, and cold, and your bed is warm and dry?

Winners of the dog days of the semester work hard during all stages of the semester. They regard the semester as a marathon, not a sprint. These students prepare consistently and make few or no excuses for their performance.

Research says: 45 percent of students at a major urban Southeastern university who had GPAs between 1.75 and 2.00 warned incoming freshmen to "keep up with assignments."[1]

At the end of my workday, which may be as late as 10 P.M., I often walk through the college library to see how many students are in the computer lab. Few students work on the computers late at night during the dog days of the semester. If I see my students in there during the dog days, I congratulate them and encourage them to keep up the good work. During the library-camper time of the semester, you cannot get a seat in those computer labs. The library campers oust the regulars. I studied at the library at UConn on a regular basis but I disliked the last two weeks of the semester because the library campers stole my spot. I think you want to be a regular and not a library camper.

Falling behind exerts a negative cumulative effect on your well-being.

You will tire during the semester. Becoming tired and run down is inevitable because the semester is stressful and its many activities steal your energy. You will become even more tired and stressed if you work from behind. Falling behind exerts a negative cumulative effect on your well-being. You become more tired as you attempt to combat the avalanche. Those who fall behind frequently pull the infamous all-nighter to study for one exam. After they have taken the test, they have to pull another all-nighter to finish a paper or study for another exam the next day. Some students go for days without sleeping. I asked the students in three of my classes if they ever studied all night. I think about three of sixty-five students had never pulled an all-nighter. I never pulled an all-nighter and you should not have to, either.

"I never pulled an all-nighter either."
—former student, graduated with a 3.5 GPA

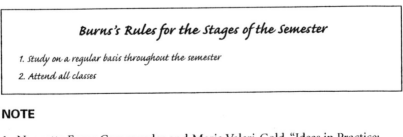

Burns's Rules for the Stages of the Semester

1. Study on a regular basis throughout the semester
2. Attend all classes

NOTE

1. Nannette Evans Commander and Maria Valeri-Gold, "Ideas in Practice: Letters of Advice from At-Risk Students to Freshmen," *Journal of Developmental Education* 27, no. 1 (2003): 28–30, 32, 34.

5

Study Habits

Make Studying a Habit

In the movie *Back to School*, Rodney Dangerfield's character, a high school dropout, tells his son that he always dreamed of going to college . . . when he fell asleep in high school. I did not pay much attention to my schoolwork in high school but I listened when teachers spoke about college. I remember one of my high school teachers saying he never pulled an all-nighter. He argued that all-nighters were not necessary. He went on to explain that our principal and a few other people he knew also did not study all night in college. My teacher's implicit argument was that all-nighters signal poor study habits and time-management skills, and that studying all night did not have to be part of the college experience. After more than fifteen years in higher education, I agree with my teacher—all-nighters are not necessary and they are signs that your study habits and time-management skills need significant improvement.

Another sign of inadequate study habits occurs when students miss one class in order to study for exams in or write papers for another course. A student once told me that he could not attend my 8:00 A.M. class because he needed to study for a 9:30 exam. He presented his case as if skipping a class to study for a test in another class was an acceptable practice. The best students attend all their classes and study well enough in advance so that they do not feel compelled to miss a class in order to cram for an exam.

Certain aspects of study habits vary from person to person. How different people take notes, read and outline books, and plan their day will differ to some degree. People possess different learning styles and preferences that shape how they approach schoolwork and studying. In the next few chapters, I explain how and where I studied and why. You may want to organize your notes in a way that differs from mine, you may like to study in your room whereas I did not, and you may prefer studying at night. Also, your style of taking notes may vary from mine because you may want to write on the right side of the page rather than left.

A good part of the next few chapters deals with concrete concepts rather than style. While your style of note taking may differ from mine, the concept is that you need to develop a system of taking notes that allows you to learn and study. While your system of organization may differ from mine, the concept is that you need to develop a way to organize your class materials that allows you to learn and study. While your study location may differ from that of others, the concept is that you need to have a place that allows you to learn and study.

Other parts of the upcoming chapters deal with rules that apply across learning styles and personal preferences. Students need to develop regular life and study patterns and they must attend all classes.[1] They must reflect on their studies in order to fully learn and appreciate the subject material.

Research says: 43 percent of students at a major urban Southeastern university who had GPAs between 1.75 and 2.00 warned incoming freshmen to "develop good study habits."[2]

To the best of my memory, I never studied much past 10:00 P.M. My study habits and time-management skills, most of which I developed in college, allowed me to outrun the avalanche. I did study at 7:00 A.M. because I was freshest at this time. I loved opening the library on the weekends because I felt like I was getting ahead of all my peers who were sleeping off their Friday nights. In reality, I *was* getting ahead. You will probably want to study at different times than I did, but you need to identify those times during which you learn and absorb the most. Furthermore, you want to study on a regular basis.

ATTEND CLASS ON A REGULAR BASIS

Class attendance is nonnegotiable. You should attend every class during the semester. Some students tell me that they missed *only* four classes during the semester. In a Tuesday/Thursday schedule, four misses equals two weeks' worth of classes. Two weeks! Certainly, your employer would fire you if you missed work for two weeks without a valid excuse.

The purpose of college is to learn. You cannot fully learn if you indiscriminately miss class.

I provide extra points to students who attend classes to which few come. I hope they understand that I want to positively reinforce their behavior. In my sophomore year in college, I took an English class with Milton Stern, who snapped when students disrespected the academic process. Class was held in an auditorium with an upper and lower level divided by a walkway. Stern yelled at students who left class early. He asked why they attended class in the first place. Stern also taught me about what I call the pack-up shuffle, which occurs when students put their books away in a loud fashion in order to end class early. He hated this move. He demanded that students never do this.

Research says: 43 percent of students at a major urban Southeastern university who had GPAs between 1.75 and 2.00 warned incoming freshmen to not miss any classes.[3]

If memory serves correctly, during my sophomore year, UConn held classes until noon on the Wednesday before Thanksgiving. Stern's class of about 150 students was nearly empty. He was furious. He told us that day's lecture would be our essay question on the final exam and he encouraged us to not provide notes to those who missed class. Stern reinforced my good behavior, and I try to do the same for my students. You always want to be in class when few attend. Anyone can attend the first day, when they feel like it, or the day before the final.

Others say, "Student complaints about mandatory attendance often center on the argument 'If I do well on the test, why do I have to come to class?' The assumption is that everything taught in a course is testable, measurable, and assessable."[4]

IMPORTANCE OF ORGANIZATION

Organization greatly helps you handle a semester. How you organize depends upon personal preferences, but organization makes learning and your life a lot easier. I kept a separate notebook and folder for each class. I used different colors for each course. I used a red notebook and folder for one course and a blue notebook and folder for another. At the beginning of each semester, I went into the UConn Co-op to buy notebooks and folders that had the university seal on the cover. You do not have to be *that* anal retentive, but I sent a strong message to myself about the importance of organization and attention to detail. To this day, I have difficulties with organization. Sometimes my office looks like a bomb hit it and I struggle to find articles and other materials from time to time. Knowing these limitations, I pay great attention to organization.

Research says: 30 percent of students at a major urban Southeastern university who had GPAs between 1.75 and 2.00 warned incoming freshmen to "stay organized."[5]

Each notebook contained a different subject, and I tried to not write my English notes in my history notebook and vice versa. I labeled each notebook on the upper left corner. For instance, I wrote, "ENGL-100-27" on the upper left corner of my English notebook. I overemphasized organization.

Materials the professor handed out went into my folder. I dated the handouts and my notes. I put the syllabus for the course in the folder. I prefer notebooks to binders with loose-leaf paper. The pages almost always stay intact in a spiral notebook. Loose-leaf pages are loose! They come out and you may lose them. Some professors, like Stern, may ask essay questions based on one lecture. It would be terrible to have taken good notes only to lose them.

Recently, as I was lecturing, I needed to look at the syllabus, and I asked one of the best students if I could see her syllabus. She opened her book bag and I noticed notebooks and folders in three different colors. Within seconds, the student produced her syllabus. This level of organization helps students handle the chaos that university life creates.

REGULAR PATTERNS

During the semester, you want to establish regular patterns of eating, sleeping, and studying. You do not want to fade or need to mount a comeback during the semester. You want to attend all of your classes. You can miss class if you get sick or if a special occasion arises, but you should not miss more than two classes in any course.

I developed a study schedule during the first week of each semester. I maintained consistent study patterns. Certainly, there were times when I needed to study more hours and a few times when I let up, but for the most part I kept regular patterns. For me, a typical week included studying Sunday through Wednesday from 7 P.M. to 10 P.M. I also stole study hours between classes. For instance, if one class ended at 11 A.M. and my next course began at 2 P.M., I ate lunch and then studied for an hour. I studied on several Thursday nights during the semester; I would not lie. I felt like I was beating my peers who were out at the bars. I tried to take

Friday and Saturday night off, but I studied on those nights when things grew more intense. I remember trying to study from about 10 A.M. to 6 P.M. on Saturdays. I believe the main library was open only during those hours. As I said earlier, there were semiregular occasions when I studied early on Saturday morning. On special occasions, I would visit a friend at another school or take the weekend off after a few exams in one week, but for the most part I kept a schedule similar to the one laid out here.

"Studying in between courses—even for a half an hour or an hour—allows students to accomplish more without studying past 10 P.M."
—former student with a 3.3 GPA

Ultimately, you must match your study rhythms to the tempo of university life, and you need to be aware of various obstacles that can prevent you from studying and learning.[6] Late-night studying presents problems that do not exist earlier in the day. For instance, the library and other study areas are less crowded and less social at 9 A.M. than they are at 9 P.M. For the most part, college parties take place around 10 P.M., not 10 A.M. Students are also more likely to experience peer pressure to go out at night than they are in the morning.

Once you make a studying schedule, you must stick to it. Students must understand that one night of partying can wreck the rest of their week. One student told me that in the early days of his college career, he would overdo it (read: drink too much) one night, thereby causing him to miss classes and studying for a few days. Several of these episodes caused him to get avalanched.

Students must realize that their activities in one day or night affect their performance in the next few days and nights. Therefore, with your class and preparation schedules firmly in mind, you need to set a time for your night to end and you must adhere to that plan. College students encounter significant peer pressure, which occurs when friends badger you to go out even though you have a paper to write or a test the next day. Remember, you must complete your work, and in order to accomplish this goal you must often resist these temptations.

Drinking and going out are not the only reasons for student absence or lack of effort. Many students do not have adequate study skills and waste too much time by hanging out. The area in front of the library served as a major place for social gatherings at one of the schools with which I have been associated, and many students lost precious time by sitting there for hours. You want to be cognizant of your time, which is more limited than you might think.

In addition to regular study patterns, you also want to develop regular life patterns. It is a good idea to have a schedule and routine that you follow consistently. As the semester unfolded, I created regular eating and sleeping patterns. On Tuesdays and Thursday, I might have a class that started at 9:30 A.M., so I ate breakfast before class, attended two classes, and then went to lunch. On Monday, Wednesday, and Friday, my day might have started later, so I kept a different schedule on these days. On most days of the semester, I knew when I was going to eat, study, and sleep. The schedule might change from time to time, but I developed a consistent pattern.

On many occasions, I see students who lack a schedule or pattern. They simply wake up and decide what to do on that day. It seems to me that these students have failed to adjust to university life. I think it is difficult to have no a plan of attack. In my view, time management becomes easier if you have a schedule. Schedules are similar to financial budgets. For a financial budget, you figure out how much money you earn, how much you spend, and then develop a plan to make sure you expend less than you take home. For a schedule, you need to determine how much time you have and how much time it will take to study. Take a conservative approach when estimating the amount of time you will need to complete your work. Better to finish early than to run out of time. As your academic career progresses, you will gain more experience and have a better idea of how much time it takes to fully learn.

TIME MANAGEMENT

The establishment of regular life and study patterns helps your time management. Time is the most important factor in time management. Of course, you say—but most students spend too little time on their schoolwork. When you begin your semester, you need to allocate significant amounts of time to studying.

Research says: 46 percent of students at a major urban Southeastern university who had GPAs between 1.75 and 2.00 warned incoming freshmen to "learn time-management skills."[7]

Two axioms I developed throughout my college career were "I have more time than I think" and "I have less time than I think." Let me explain these phrases. On many occasions, I did not think I had enough time to finish my papers or to study for exams. At Thanksgiving, I would say that there was no way I could do all my assignments before the end of the semester, but I always did. In graduate school, I freaked out over time. I wanted to obtain my doctorate in four years and I did not think that was possible. I remember expressing this concern to a mentor of mine, who told me, "You have more time than you think." He was correct, and I finished in four years. So remember, whenever you think you have too little time, you probably have more time than you think.

At times, you will hit a stretch where you either procrastinate or you have so much to do that you do not know where to start. When these situations occur, you should do something. When procrastination sets in, get to the computer and start writing. Do something. I often found that making a to-do list of all the things I had to do helped settle my mind.

Once they are written, however, you must act on the lists you made. In graduate school, my friend took comprehensive exams that consisted of answering three questions over a five-day period. After the second day, to-do lists and outlines were the only things she wrote. I encouraged her to start writing her essays and stop making lists, because she was more than prepared to answer the questions. By the end of the next day, she had finished all three questions. She needed a little encouragement in order to start.

Research says, "Participants' reasons for procrastinating when given a scenario concerning writing a term paper were varied: 78.3% endorsed 'Just felt too lazy to write a term paper'. . . . Items that were endorsed by at least 20% of respondents included: 'Friends were pressuring you to do other things,' 'Felt overwhelmed by the task,' 'Felt it just takes too long to write a term paper,' 'Did not have enough energy to begin the task,' 'Really disliked writing term papers,' 'Were concerned that you would not meet your own expectations,' and 'Worried that you would get a bad grade.'"[8]

To this day, I make to-do lists and I feel a great sense of accomplishment when I scratch items off the list. When I was a college student, however, there was a period of time in which I would study all day and never scratch anything off the to-do list. This experience discouraged me. My father came to visit during this time and I explained the situation to him. He liked the idea of the to-do list but he encouraged me to reflect on how much I accomplished at the end of the day irrespective of the to-do list. For instance, I might have five things on the to-do list and I accomplished five things not on the to-do list. By looking only at the to-do list, it appeared as if I had done nothing. By reflecting on the amount of work I accomplished, I could see my achievements. I continue this practice to this day.

Many times, students believe they have more time than they actually have. This phenomenon often occurs during spring break and on long weekends. Students think they will catch up on everything during these periods, but they overestimate the time they have and underestimate the amount of work. Make sure that you set reasonable expectations for what you can accomplish because you may have less time than you think.

HARD STUFF FIRST

As a general rule, you should study the subjects you do not like before you concentrate on the ones you prefer. While you may perform better in and like one subject more than another, the courses to which you do not pay attention can hurt your performance in other courses. For instance, if you ignore math until the week of an exam, your preparation for a history test, which is the same day, may be affected negatively. As Thomas McQueeney, my high school teacher and one of my early mentors, said, focus first on those subjects you dislike. If you study the subjects you prefer first, you are more likely to ignore other, less appealing subjects when you grow tired. As you tire, you want to study the subjects you like, not those you do not. Furthermore, it is easy to study and perform well in subjects that you like. As I wrote earlier, true learners study all subjects, including and especially those they dislike.

As a general rule, you should study the subjects you do not like before you focus upon the ones you prefer. While you will perform better in and like one subject more than another, the courses to which you do not pay attention hurt your performance in other courses.

WHERE TO STUDY?

Find a place to study that is right for you. I studied primarily in the library. For the most part, the library was conducive to studying. The basement of the Babbidge Library at UConn got a little too social and loud from time to time, but the fourth floor was quiet during the semester. I studied in the library because other students who were also trying to learn surrounded me. The university library, especially the upper floors, is full of committed students, and that environment facilitates learning. The library provides few distractions. I am a television and telephone bandit. When I tried to study in my dorm room, I concentrated for a short time but then made phone calls and watched television. You can hide in the library. I went to little corners of the library where no one could spot me. Other times, I wanted to be a little more social, so I moved to the basement to chat with friends.

In your dorm room, you cannot escape your friends who come in to see you. You must coordinate your study schedule with your roommate, who may like to watch television, play music or video games, or invite friends over. I used my dorm room and my home as places to rest and relax. It was nice to know that I could unwind in my room when I returned from the library.

T-H-I-N-K

You need to reflect on your studies. I tell students to turn on their minds. I encourage them to think about their classes, readings, assignments, and studies. College provides so many distractions that take students' attention away from studying. Many students give in to these distractions and they never think seriously about their studies. I encourage you to spend time thinking about and contemplating each of your subjects. When I reflected on my subjects, I went to a corner of the library and literally laid out my notes and the syllabus. I asked myself, "What is the professor trying to communicate? What are the major points or themes the professor communicates in class and through the readings?" I thought about these questions for a few minutes and used my notes and the readings to answer these questions. These reflection sessions added clarity to my studies. If I did not understand one point, I asked my professor detailed questions during office hours. I always wanted to know what the class was supposed to know and what we were going to learn. Your grades and learning should improve once you think about the significance and direction of the lectures and readings.

When I reflected on my subjects, I went to a corner of the library and literally laid out my notes and the syllabus. I asked myself, "What is the professor trying to communicate? What are the major points or themes the professor communicates in class and through the readings?" I thought about these questions for a few minutes and I used my notes and the readings to answer these questions. These reflection sections added clarity to my studies.

On some occasions, college distractions assist students, especially ones who study all the time. At times, students need to turn their minds off. During my college career, I needed to move away from my studies in order to get a fresh perspective. As my father said to me when he told me to put my books down for a while, "You need to recharge. That's why they have halftime in football. You cannot exert that much pressure on your body and mind without giving them a rest." In my college career, I found that I accomplished much more when I was rested than I did when I was tired. It amazed me when I quickly read one chapter at the beginning of the day when I was fresh whereas I got through only one more chapter during the rest of the day as I grew tired.

Burns's Rules for Studying

1. Dedicate significant time to your studies
2. Organization greatly helps students handle semesters
3. Attend every class
4. Develop regular life and study patterns
5. Study your hardest subjects first
6. Find a place where you can concentrate on your studies
7. Reflect on your studies

General Tips for Studying

1. Color coordinate notebooks and folders for each class

2. How you structure your time and set your specific schedules is a personal preference

3. The library is a good place to study

NOTES

1. I tell my students to avoid absolutes, such as *never* and *always*. However, I truly believe that all students need to have a plan of attack for the semester and attendance of all classes is vital.

2. Commander and Valeri-Gold, "Ideas in Practice."

3. Commander and Valeri-Gold, "Ideas in Practice."

4. Holly Hassel and Jessica Lourey, "The Dea(r)th of Student Responsibility," *College Teaching* 53, no. 1 (2005): 2–13.

5. Commander and Valeri-Gold, "Ideas in Practice."

6. For this information, I am indebted to Matthew O. Thomas.

7. Commander and Valeri-Gold, "Ideas in Practice."

8. Mera M. Kachgal, Sunny L. Hansen, and Kevin J. Nutter, "Academic Procrastination Prevention/Intervention: Strategies and Recommendations," *Journal of Developmental Education* 25, no. 1 (2001): 14–21.

6

Advice on Exams

Prepare, Don't Cram

You cannot follow the advice in this chapter if you do not work in advance. The advice in this book helps only those who really want to succeed. If you prepare in advance, these tips will help you to learn and, hopefully, secure a better grade. The approach you take may vary from mine, but you should follow the basic principles of advance preparation, understanding what the exam will cover, paying attention to detail, and studying the notes and the readings.

The most common exams are multiple choice, essay, and short answers or identifications.[1] Some professors may also use true-or-false and fill-in-the-blanks. Multiple-choice exams ask students to select the correct answer from four or five alternatives. Short-answer or identification questions require students to provide specific information on a particular topic. Students need to address the significance of the short answers or identifications. Beyond *who*, *what*, *where*, and *when*, *why* is the topic of this question important and *how* does this topic affect the overall subject area. If an exam asks you to identify James Madison, then you should include relevant facts about Madison, including that he wrote the Constitution, was member of the original House of Representatives, and served as the fourth president of the United States. Beyond these facts, Madison is significant partly because his ideas about separation of powers and checks and balances shaped the Constitution and affect government and politics today.

To answer essay questions, students must provide both facts and independent analyses of several topics. In the sample essay question in Figure 6.1, students must define the American political culture and all its parts. Then they must apply each of the six aspects of the American political culture to a contemporary issue. As you can see, the answer for this question will be more detailed and contain more analysis than would the answer for the identification of James Madison.

Many professors use an array of these methods in one test. For example, one exam might include multiple-choice questions, short answers, and an essay. Students may have choices when they take essay exams. Some professors provide five essay topics and students need to answer three of these questions.

FIGURE 6.1
Sample Essay Question

Please answer the following question. Please define each element of the American political culture. Which aspects apply to this concept, which do not, and why?

If you make the case that an aspect of the American political culture does not apply to an issue area, then please be quite certain that this concept is not relevant. You need to clearly explain why each concept does or does not apply. Please use proper grammar, which includes complete sentences and action verbs. 50 points

The progressive tax "increases as the amount to be taxed increases. For example, a taxing authority might levy a tax of 10% on the first $10,000 of income and increase the rate by 5% per each $10,000 increment up to a maximum of 50% on all income over $80,000. A progressive tax often uses high rates on relatively large incomes and tends to encourage tax shelters. The federal income tax, many state income taxes, and the unified gift-estate tax are progressive taxes."[2] How does the progressive tax reflect (or not reflect) the American political culture?

In Figure 6.2, you will see a typical exam I use in my Introduction to American Government course. I provide choices to students on the identifications but I require students to answer the essay. Students need to make sure that they explain the significance of the identifications and they must answer each part of the essay question.

When I attended the University of Connecticut, many of my professors used multiple-choice exams in the large introductory classes. In my upper-level (junior and senior) courses, professors relied on a combination of short answers/identifications, essays, and papers (see Figure 6.3).

FIGURE 6.2
Sample Exam, Introduction to American Government (primarily a course for first-year students)

Identifications
You must define and explain the significance of five (5) of the following six. Each answer is worth 10 points.

1. What is James Madison's thesis in *Federalist 51*? How does the American Government embody the ideas Madison expresses in this article? Please provide specifics to support your answer.
2. Shays' Rebellion
3. What is Alexis de Tocqueville's thesis in "Origins and Democratic Social Conditions of the Anglo-Americans?"
4. Describe the procedure to amend the Constitution
5. Government and politics
6. Equality of opportunity and equality of result

Essay
Please answer the following question, worth 50 points.
    What is a constitution? What are the national government's constitutional powers? Why does the national government possess these powers? What role do majority rule and minority rights play in the new constitution and why? Who were the Federalists and Anti-Federalists? What did they think about the new constitution? How did they shape the new constitution?

FIGURE 6.3
Sample Final Exam, Introduction to International Relations (class that consists
primarily of college sophomores)[3]

PART 1: *Map Identification.* Identify the country, feature, or body of water that corresponds with the number on the maps. (1 point each)

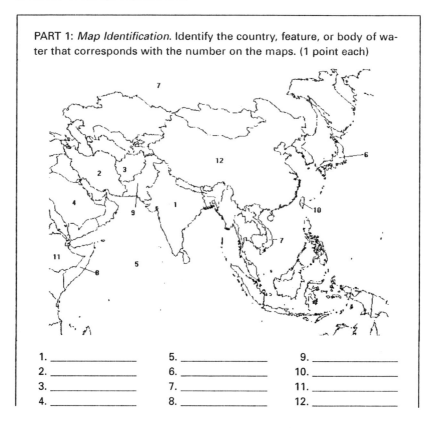

1. _____   5. _____   9. _____
2. _____   6. _____   10. _____
3. _____   7. _____   11. _____
4. _____   8. _____   12. _____

13. _____   16. _____   19. _____
14. _____   17. _____   20. _____
15. _____   18. _____

(*continued*)

FIGURE 6.3
Continued

PART 2: *Identification.* Define and describe the significance of thirteen of the following items, terms, or concepts in one or two sentences. (2 points each)

1. Aum Shinrikyo
2. Autarky
3. Sustainable Development
4. "Frankenfood"
5. Import Substitution
6. Hugo Grotius
7. Tiltulim
8. The Resource Curse
9. Floating Exchange Rates
10. Dirty Bombs
11. Cartels
12. Boxer Rebellion
13. The Fourteen Points
14. Structural Adjustments
15. ECOSOC

PART 3: *"Jeopardy"—Style Identification.* Provide *twelve* of the following terms or concepts that match the definitions. (2 points each) [only some sample questions provided]

1. _____ A New Hampshire town that hosted a meeting of capitalist powers in 1944 at which an economic arrangement and a number of key institutions were created that were to designed to rely on the economic strength of the United States to avert a return to economic depression.

2. _____ The concept at the heart of economic liberalism's faith in free trade. Proponents of this concept argue that every nation has certain inherent economic strengths that can be exploited to create wealth.

3. _____ A concept borrowed from group psychology that can be seen as an impediment to rational decision making, this term describes the ten-

dency for people in groups to act more reck-
lessly and less cautiously than they would alone.

4. _____ The behavior by which decision makers are
content to select an alternative that meets
minimally acceptable standards rather than
continuing to seek an optimal solution.

5. _____ This theory suggests that war is likely when a
country rises in relative power compared to its
neighbors, because those neighboring countries often calculate that that war "sooner"
would be better than war "later."

6. _____ One of the key insights of this alternative view
of human rationality is that "losing hurts twice
as bad as winning feels good."

7. _____ An NGO that was founded in order to raise
awareness of (and ultimately influence international policy regarding) the debt crisis in many
of the countries of the Global South.

8. _____ Often called the "essence of statehood," this is
the right of a state to control events inside its
borders free of outside interference.

PART 4: *Short Answers.* Answer all parts of the following questions.
(5 points each)

1. What are the four components of the "Powell Doctrine"? Did the
   wars with Iraq satisfy those components?
2. What differentiates the function of loans from the World Bank from
   those of the IMF? Give a hypothetical example of the kinds of loan
   that each institution would make.
3. Explain the difference between peacekeeping and peace enforce-
   ment, and give a real-world example of each.
4. What are the two major classifications of biological weapons? What
   is the difference between the two? Give an example of each.
5. What are the four generally recognized sources of modern international law?
6. Explain the difference between what we have termed micro- and
   macrolevel feminism, and give an example (real or hypothetical) of
   the kinds of issues with which each deals.

(continued)

FIGURE 6.3
Continued

---

7. Explain the difference between "Cornucopians" and "Neo-
   Malthusians." Pick one issue of concern to international environmen-
   talists, and (briefly) explain how the two schools of thought would
   approach the issue.
8. What was the founding principle of the League of Nations? What
   were the founding principles of the Charter of the United Nations?
   Why did the former fail?

PART 5: *Essays.* Answer all parts of one of the following questions.
(20 points)

1. One of the key puzzles that scholars of international relations have
   tried to explain is the outbreak of war. Why does war happen? Explain at least *six* of the potential causes of war that we have discussed in class. Be sure to explain at least one from each of the three
   levels of analysis in international relations.
2. In class we have discussed many visions of the future of the international system. Discuss *four* of those visions. What do the visions
   project? Who first articulated them? From what school of thought in
   international relations do they seem to emerge? Finally, which vision
   do you find to be most convincing? Which do you find least convincing? Why?

Multiple-choice tests were much less common in my upper-level
courses.

At smaller colleges, students are more likely to have short answers/
identifications, essays, and papers in their freshman and sophomore years.
The smaller class size allows professors to grade these exams whereas the
larger class size at public universities makes multiple-choice exams a more
viable option for professors there. As a professor, I do not give multiple-
choice tests. Instead, I primarily use papers and short answers, identifications, and essay tests to evaluate students. In my upper-division courses, I
assign large research papers that are between fifteen and twenty-five pages
in length (for more on paper writing, see chapter 7).

For two of my political science courses at the University of Connecticut, twice a week I attended a large lecture with the entire class, and for the third class I was in a so-called discussion section with a teaching assistant and about thirty students. As a teaching assistant at Maryland and at UConn, I led these discussion sections. As a student, I used these sessions to clarify parts of the lecture I did not understand. Many students think that the teaching assistants will provide clues about what is on the exam, but I must caution you against this assumption. Many teaching assistants have no idea what will be on the exam. At Maryland, the professor made up the exam and did not even let the teaching assistants see the exam before the test date. At UConn, I helped make the exam but only after all the discussion classes were over. Therefore, I could not provide hints about the contents of the exam during discussion sessions.

Professors may also assign take-home and open-book exams. Do not underestimate the difficulty of these kinds of exams. For take-home exams, students must answer three to five questions and return the test in two to three days. The take-home exam, which needs to be typed, is more detailed than an essay test but less detailed than a paper.

To prepare for a take-home exam, I suggest that you make an inventory of the information that may be on the exam. The inventory of information will help you prepare for take-home exams. Outlines of notes and readings should separate the major topics and subtopics covered on the test (see Figure 6.4). The more details you can incorporate into your outline, the easier it will be to write the take-home essay. In the mini-outline below, you can see how the details about the president's domestic powers

FIGURE 6.4
Sample Outline

1. President's Domestic Powers
   a. Veto
   b. State of the Union Address
2. Media

allow the writer to answer a question on this topic. An even better outline would include more powers and particulars about the origins of powers and how the president exercises his authority. Once you have the test, you want to spend most of the time organizing your answer and writing. You do not want to spend much time researching the answer. The research should occur before you receive the test.

Professors' expectations are much higher for take-home exams than they are for in-class tests. Professors want more detailed answers for take-home exams. They also may expect you to use outside sources for take-home exams, whereas they would not require you to utilize such information for in-class tests.

I find open-book tests to be a bit of a trap. Students may think that they do not have to study because they can use their books or even their notes during the test. My suggestion would be to study for an open-book test in the same way you prepare for a closed-book test. Additionally, for open-book tests I organized my books and my notes in such a way that I could readily access information on various topics. For instance, I might put Post-it notes on the top of some pages and write something like "information on presidential powers," on the note. That way, I could quickly get the information I needed.

Like everything else, advance preparation is the key to studying for exams and writing papers. You need to know the due dates of all exams and papers in order to work ahead. In regard to studying for exams, you need to know which material the exam covers. Your syllabus and the professor provide the best sources for this information. Read your syllabus to see if it specifies which chapters and topics will be covered in the exam. If the syllabus is unclear, ask the professor detailed questions about the exam. Professors do not like to hear, "Will this be on the exam?" because this question suggests you only care about grades. However, you can ask the professor about the topics and reading assignments that will appear on the exam. Most professors will answer these questions.

Professors do not like to hear, "Will this be on the exam?" because this question suggests you care only about grades.

Once you know what the exam covers, you want to make an inventory of the information that may be on the test. You must identify which lecture dates will be on the exam. Identification of the class readings that may be on the exam constitutes an essential part of studying for a test. You want to make sure you study all of the material that will be on the exam. Too often, students cannot answer exam questions because they did not study that particular material. You can avoid this trap or at least mitigate this possibility by knowing and studying the material upon which the test is based.

Others say, "Regular reviews are the key to reducing test anxiety and taking tests successfully. Frequent review is very important. Creating review tools such as flashcards, chapter outlines, and summaries will help the student organize and remember material. Another useful tool is a study checklist."[4]

I think you should start to prepare for the exam at least two weeks before the test date. Attack your notes. Professors lecture upon topics that interest them. In their lectures, professors often discuss what they believe to be the most important subjects in their field. The lecture material will often, but not always, represent one part of the exam. You should consult your notes soon after each class. This method further familiarizes you with the information. It enables you to figure out which parts of the lecture you do not understand, and it should allow you to determine the main themes of the lectures.

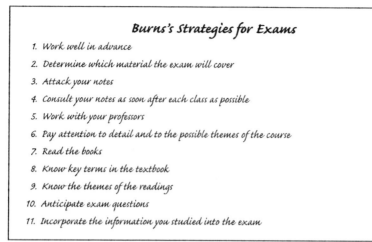

Burns's Strategies for Exams

1. Work well in advance

2. Determine which material the exam will cover

3. Attack your notes

4. Consult your notes as soon after each class as possible

5. Work with your professors

6. Pay attention to detail and to the possible themes of the course

7. Read the books

8. Know key terms in the textbook

9. Know the themes of the readings

10. Anticipate exam questions

11. Incorporate the information you studied into the exam

You should work with your professors in order to learn (see more about this in chapter 9). If holes exist in your notes, then you need to ask the professor to clarify these points. When you go to a professor's office hours, you accomplish several important tasks. You clarify important aspects of the exam, you show the professor you care, and, most importantly, you learn more than you would have had you not made use of the office hours.

Others say: In giving test-taking advice to kids, one educational administrator suggested that, *before* the test, students should

1. "study on a regular basis"

2. "know exactly what the test will cover"

3. "do not stay up all night before the test to study"

4. "study in small groups"

5. "be prepared"

6. "come to the test with a positive attitude"

7. "listen to all oral directions carefully."[5]

You need to pay attention to detail. The lectures provide insight into important themes. These themes are often important parts of the exam. Remember, you must move beyond the facts, that is, who, what, where, and when, in order to address why and how.

You must move beyond the facts, that is, *who, what, where,* and *when,* in order to address the *why* and *how.*

Studying class readings is often difficult work. If you read a textbook, then I would focus upon a few things. Most textbooks set key terms in boldface, and I tried to understand these concepts. I outlined each chapter, and asked myself, "What am I supposed to learn from this chapter?" An answer to this question provides an idea of which kinds of questions the professor can ask from the book. If available, you should study the index of each chapter. Many textbooks outline the chapters and this formal structure enables you to better understand the main points of each chapter. I also linked the readings to the lectures. How do the readings complement what the professor says? Which lessons do the readings teach that the lectures have not covered? Some overlap should exist between the readings but also concentrate on those readings that present new material.

Highlighter pens never helped me much, but I think you should try them. They distracted me and prolonged my reading without any benefits of retention, but my experience may differ from yours. I used a regular pen and bracketed the text and points I found to be important. I also made notes in the margins and these comments aided me greatly.

Research says, "College students who want to use highlighting as a study technique should purchase books that are not previously highlighted for two reasons. (1) Previous highlighting may be confused with their highlighting, and (2) pre-existing appropriate highlighting is not beneficial to the student; only if the student is actively involved in the highlighting process will the student profit from this study technique."[6]

If tests focus upon nontextbook readings then you should summarize the thesis or main points of each chapter and the book. You can search for these points in the introduction and concluding chapter. The chapters in the middle support these points. Students often drown in a tidal wave of facts, and you want to avoid this trap. Instead, you want to isolate the book's thesis and how the authors support their points. If you work far enough in advance, you can hold a discussion with the professor about what you regard as the main points of the book.

Students often drown in a tidal wave of facts, and you want to avoid this fate.

Once you have completed all this studying, you want to use this information on the exam. I watch too many students prepare for the exam but not use the information they have learned. I tell the students, "More is more." Do not make things up or embellish, but use all the materials to answer the questions. Use your inventory to show the professor what you have learned. The use of all or most of your inventory demonstrates how hard you worked, how much you prepared, and how much you learned. If you do not use what you studied, then the content of your test will not be much different from that of those who did not study, and your grade on the exam will not reflect how much you learned.

I found it to be helpful to anticipate the exam questions. The lectures and the themes of the class often provide the basis for essay questions. You can prepare for essay exams by thinking about how you would answer various questions based on the themes. I practiced this technique at the very end of my preparation period.

One theme to this section on preparation for exams, for instance, is that you need to pay attention to detail. If you pay attention to detail, you can anticipate the questions on the exam. If you pay attention to detail, you can write a well-thought-out and complete essay. If you pay attention to detail, you will better understand the material and how to learn it.

When you take an essay exam, I advise you to write clearly. You need to clearly communicate your points to the professor. One way to accomplish this goal is to make an outline before you write. You want structure in your essay, which needs to be well written. In line with this advice, always use proper grammar and fully spell out words. Many teachers do not tolerate sloppy essays or abbreviated words. Clear penmanship adds clarity to your exam. Like a term paper, your essay should include an introduction, a body, and a conclusion. It should have a thesis that you support with evidence. Many students include facts in their essays, but they do not include a thesis and a conclusion, which set excellent exams apart from the rest.

Others say, "On essay questions, make a time schedule to allow you to answer all the questions (if there are five questions to answer in 60 minutes, allow 12 minutes per question). When answers come to mind immediately for a question, jot down key words or concepts while they are fresh in your mind. Think before the pen touches the paper. Make a brief outline or graphic organizer for each question. Get right to the point by stating your main point in the first sentence."[7]

Multiple-choice exams are difficult, and advice abounds about them. Some people have told me to stick with my first choice or try to choose the answer unlike the others. The best advice I can give about multiple-choice tests is to select the answer that most completely answers the question. Many answers look right and some will be partially correct. You want the one that is fully correct. You need to concentrate and know the material. Attention to detail is key. Slowly read each question. The wording of the question is essential. You need to understand the meaning of and pay attention to words such as *or, always,* and *but.* Slowly answer each question. Your mind can play tricks on you because you will quickly read the question and anticipate the answer. Sometimes professors devise questions so that students incorrectly anticipate the answer.

Others say, "On multiple-choice questions, eliminate the possible answers that are obviously wrong. . . . Make a note of qualifying words such as *often*, *generally*, *usually*, *seldom*, and *may*. Such qualifiers could indicate a true statement. Note such superlatives as *only*, *every*, *always*, *none*, and *all*. These words indicate that the correct answer is an undisputed fact. In social sciences, absolutes are rare."[8]

Once you have completed the exam, I strongly recommend that you recheck your answers. Resist the temptation to leave the exam once you are done. By taking some time to review your exam, you can save yourself many points. I always tried to use all the time the professor allotted for the exam. As long as you answer the questions in a thorough and complete manner, then it does not matter how long you take to finish the exam. I have not systematically studied this issue, but I notice that many of the best students take most, if not all, of the time allotted, and many not-so-good students tend to be among the first to turn in their exams.

Others say, "On true/false questions, be wary of words such as *always*, *never*, and *only*. These words place heavy restrictions on the statement. If you can think of a single exception, then the answer is false. Remember that every part of a true sentence must be true."[9]

Making mistakes is part of life. Making the same mistakes over and over is a crime (see chapter 12 for more on assessment). You need to evaluate your exams and papers once the professor returns them. Improvement comes only if you determine why you made mistakes. Which kinds of mistakes did you make? Did the multiple choices deceive you? Did you miss the questions on the lectures or on the book? Did you write a strong essay? You need to determine the reasons for your mistakes and create a game plan to correct them. I would take your exam to the professor about one week after the test and ask how you can improve. You do not want to talk to the professor directly after the exam, because you may still be upset with your grade, and you might say something you do not mean. Wait to talk to the teacher (for more on this subject, see the five stages of grief at the end of chapter 9).

Burns's Rules for Exams

1. *Know which topics the exam will cover*

2. *Pay attention to detail*

3. *Use the information you studied on the exam*

4. *On essay exams, write clearly and legibly*

General Tips on Exams

1. Work with your professors

2. Identify the key terms in each chapter

3. Outline the chapters

4. Summarize the thesis or main points of the chapter

5. Anticipate the exam question

6. Write an outline before you write your essay

7. Choose the multiple-choice response that most completely answers the question

---

NOTES

1. For this information, I am indebted to Matthew O. Thomas.

2. "Progressive Tax," dictionary.reference.com/search?q=progressive%20tax.

3. For this information, I am indebted to Christopher J. Fettweis.

4. Diane Loulou, "How to Study for and Take College Tests," ACCESS ERIC (Washington, DC: Office of Educational Research and Improvement [ED], 1997).

5. Robert E. Glenn. "Teach Kids Test-Taking Tactics," *Education Digest* 70, no. 2 (1997): 61–64.

6. Vicki L. Silvers and David S. Kreiner, "The Effects of Pre-Existing Inappropriate Highlighting on Reading Comprehension," *Reading Research and Instruction* 36 (Spring 1997): 217–23.

7. Glenn, "Teach Kids Test-Taking Tactics."

8. Glenn, "Teach Kids Test-Taking Tactics."

9. Glenn, "Teach Kids Test-Taking Tactics."

7

Paper Writing

Build a Tasty and Well-Presented Cake

Think of writing a paper or an essay as tantamount to building a cake. Like a tasty cake, the essay must contain the best ingredients. The more you study, the more relevant information (ingredients) you can include in your essay. More attention to detail leads to better essays. Excellent papers include much more than facts. To write an excellent paper, you must present a well-constructed argument. Like the cake, the essay answer must look good and have substance. A good-looking, substantive paper includes a thesis, an introduction, a body, and a conclusion. Each section of a good paper links to the other. The extra attention to detail resembles the icing and a cherry on top, but you should beware of spending too much time on the icing and not enough on the cake. One of my friends often studied the obscure graphs and maps in order to answer the difficult questions, but he did not know the basics.

Students need to use evidence to support their knowledge claims. A knowledge claim occurs when one makes an assertion. Christopher Columbus made a knowledge claim that the earth was round. He supported this contention by not falling off the planet. Students encounter two problems with knowledge claims. On the one hand, students make knowledge claims but they fail to use their notes, the assigned readings, or outside materials to back their assertions. If they were Columbus, they would simply say the world is round and want us to take their word for it. On the other hand, some students provide facts but never make knowledge claims. If they were Columbus, they would say they had sailed around the world, but they would not explain why this fact is important. As you write your paper, you want to use evidence to support what you assert.

Students need to use evidence to support their knowledge claims. A knowledge claim occurs when students make assertions.

In this book, I make knowledge claims about how to succeed in college. I use various sources to support these assertions. My experiences as a student, teaching assistant, professor, and adviser support my knowledge claims. The use of others' research also bolsters the assertions I make.

Writing is complicated, but the basic premise behind it is to clearly communicate points to the reader. Clarity is paramount. At some point, many students—including this one—believed that great prose is needed in order to communicate a point. In my pursuits to impress teachers, I wrote unclearly. When I wrote my dissertation, my adviser said my writing was unclear. He told me to get back to the basics by writing clear sentences, some long and some short. He suggested using Strunk and White's *Elements of Style* as a way to improve my clarity.[1] This suggestion was excellent. Another prolific writer recommended *Style: The Basics of Clarity and Grace* by Joseph M. Williams, and this book also improved my writing.[2]

Writing takes practice.

Writing is a hard process that takes time. You may want to read these books from time to time and practice your writing on a regular basis. I keep these books on my nightstand and read a chapter from time to time. I try to incorporate something I read into my writing. I impart these lessons to my students. I find these books to be helpful, but they can be overwhelming and paralyzing. Many of my better students say, "Oh my, I made all of these mistakes!" and they hesitate before writing again.[3] I tell them to get something on paper and then revise accordingly. I would work on a few paragraphs at first, and keep some basic writing rules in mind when you compose in the future. Writing takes practice. By working on my writing, I am better than I was five years ago, and with more attention to detail, I will be even better in the future. Fettweis agrees. He believes that student writing improves with every paper even though students may not realize it.

Research says: In a study of 315 freshmen at Toledo and Indiana State Universities, "one-third of the students identified writing practice as the high school activity that best prepared them for college writing."[4]

Images of my students pop into my head when I read their papers. For the best papers, I envision a student who took his or her time, collected relevant information, made an outline, wrote a draft, put the paper away, reread the paper, maybe had someone else read the paper, and then made final corrections. For the worst papers, I see students working in the middle of the night before the due date. These students write only to complete the paper. They finish their paper just as the time comes for class. When I started teaching, I had no policy regarding whether students needed to attend class on the paper's due date. During my first semester as a professor, I noticed that the worst students finished their papers during class time and turned the paper in as the class ended. I created a policy that considers papers to be late when students miss class. When students spend all night working on a paper, they tend to have many proofreading mistakes, and their papers lack focus. Time affects performance.

Burns says, "During my first semester as a professor, I noticed that the worst students finished their papers during class time and turned the paper in as the class ended."

Well-written papers take a short time to read. By contrast, poorly written papers consume much more time as I must go back and try to figure out the writer's intent. Proofreading mistakes ruin continuity.

My cardinal rule in writing papers is to avoid proofreading mistakes. Proofreading mistakes occur when students misspell words, mistype words—for instance, typing *if* when they wanted to write *it*—and generally include passages they would have eliminated had they thoroughly read their papers. Proofreading mistakes indicate you did not work on your paper in advance. They give the professor the impression that you do not care about the paper or the class. If you do not care about your work, then the professor will care even less. *Any time* you put your name on a paper, you must hand in top-quality work. Your work is a representation of you. Well-researched and well-written papers provide glowing examples of your work, whereas papers with proofreading mistakes demonstrate incompetence.

Professor Fettweis says, "Good papers are never first drafts."

Drafts are excellent ways to improve clarity and to avoid proofreading mistakes. You should ask your professors if they will read your paper in advance. If not, then you may want to take the draft to the writing center on campus. I have mixed emotions about writing centers. At one university I attended, I found the counselors to be quite condescending. One counselor told me that I needed to write topic sentences, and I replied that I had. She looked at me in amazement, and handed my paper to another counselor and said something like "He thinks there is a topic sentence in here . . ." I never returned after a few of those experiences. I think you should receive assistance from the professor, and if you work in advance, you may get it. Even providing an outline or an introductory paragraph to the teacher is an excellent start.

"Good writers get jobs and promotions. Every job requires some level of writing."

—Dr. Matthew O. Thomas

Many of my colleagues whose opinions I respect think very highly of writing centers. They believe that writing centers not only improve papers but also facilitate students' writing abilities. Because of their opinions, I encourage you to take your paper to your campus's writing center. If your writing mentor is neither friendly nor helpful, do not abandon the writing center. Many different people work at these centers and just because one person was unhelpful does not mean that all the staff and workers are that way. I would give the writing center several opportunities to help you. When you find an especially caring and supportive mentor, find out when this person works and take your papers to him or her.

Regardless of the quality of your college's writing center, these mentors neither perform miracles nor write papers. Writing centers neither make an A out of an F paper nor finish an incomplete paper. Students need to write their papers as best they can, and then take those essays to the writing center. Your paper will improve if you have time to revise it after you go to the writing center. If you wait until the last minute, you will not be able to make all the revisions necessary to write a strong paper. You also need to learn from these writing centers. Which mistakes did you make on this paper and how can you learn from these errors in the future?

Research says, "Although students worked on group projects outside of class, they seldom visited the library or made use of college skill centers."[5]

Outlines are also essential for clarity. In high school and even college, my teachers specified how to create an outline. I never forgot that you cannot have a 1 without a 2, or an A without a B. What I did not figure out until later was why I needed an outline. Outlines structure your argument. They provide purpose to your paragraphs.

Answer the essay question, and all its parts! You want to make sure that you answer the essay question and address the paper topic. Both as a student and as a professor I notice that students drift from the paper topic and write *their* paper as opposed to the one the professor wants. You want to avoid this trap.

You also need to answer all of the questions. I provide many questions for my term papers, and many students write extensively on some questions but totally skip others, and this technique costs major points. Some students also provide too much background information without answering the question, and you want to avoid this as well. One way to make sure you answer the question is to take a yellow highlighter and highlight all the sentences that directly answer the question. If the paper is predominantly yellow, then you have done your job. If not, you need to go back and directly answer the question.

Students spend too much time worrying about page length. I would concentrate on thoroughly answering the questions, and worry less about page length. If the professor provides minimum or maximum page lengths, however, then you must make certain to not fall below or go beyond these requirements.

I advise students to create an outline by first typing the assignment questions and then separating each question. Once students put the questions into outline form, they should write the answers or where they can find the answers under the relevant question. This outline ensures that you address the assignment and answer each question.

In my American Government course, I assign a paper that asks students to determine which branch of government has the most power and why. I tell the students that they must use facts to support their opinions. I also ask the students to adhere to the instructions listed in Table 7.1.

In the aforementioned assignment, students need to pay attention to the word *must*, which means that they will lose points if they do not answer this question. My outline for this assignment would look like the one in Table 7.2.

Under each number listed in Table 7.2, I would either include where I could find the answer or I would make sure I followed the criteria. For number 1, I would provide a thesis statement and evidence that sup-

Table 7.1. Sample Paper Topic

Which branch of government has the most power and why?

While this question asks for your opinion, you must support your opinion with facts. You must discuss why the branch that you selected is more powerful than the other two. This requires that you discuss and compare all three branches of government.

You must support your answer with information from the readings and the class. Do not base your answers on outside information. This is not to say that you cannot use outside sources. However, base your answers on the readings, the class, and the homework assignments.

Remember that you must support your answer with facts. The following are guidelines that you must follow in your paper:

1. Provide a thesis-type statement that lets the reader know what you are proving.
2. Consider the various components of the question before you start writing so that you base your answer on information drawn from careful consideration of the class and the readings.

The paper must be typewritten and double-spaced with margins that are at least 1" all around. The font must be 12 point. Points will be deducted if these requirements are not met. The paper can be no longer than seven (7) pages.

Please see the suggestions for writing a better paper on my website, www.loyno .edu/~pburns. You must also use either MLA Citation Style or *The Chicago Manual of Style* to cite your sources. Points will be deducted if you do not follow the writing tips and the style requirements. You will lose two points for each spelling mistake and each grammar mistake.

ports my claim that one branch has more power than the others. For number 3, I would make certain to include examples from the readings. An outline such as this one allows you to pay attention to detail and it helps provide a thorough answer to the question.

The goal of writing is to make your reader understand your point. You must strive for clarity. Papers improve when you ease the reader's ability to comprehend. Proper grammar and well-structured sentences and paragraphs make it easy for your reader to comprehend your paper. You also want to provide a blueprint that lets your reader know the direction of your paper. Many subpar papers, most of which were written just prior to the deadline, possess neither rhyme nor reason. An outline helps to properly structure your paper. For more tips on writing papers, see Table 7.3.

Table 7.2. Sample Outline of the Aforementioned Paper Topic

1. You must discuss why the branch that you selected is more powerful than the other two.
2. This requires that you discuss (and compare) all three branches of government.
3. You must support your answer with information from the readings and the class.
4. Do not base your answers on outside information.
5. This is not to say that you cannot use outside sources. However, base your answers on the readings, the class, and the homework assignments.
6. Remember that you must support your answer with facts.
7. The following are guidelines that you must follow in your paper.
   1. Provide a thesis-type statement that lets the reader know what you are proving.
   2. Consider the various components of the question before you start writing so that you base your answer on information drawn from careful consideration of the class and the readings.
8. The paper must be typewritten and double-spaced with margins that are at least 1" all around.
9. The font must be 12 point. Points will be deducted if these requirements are not met.
10. The paper can be no longer than seven (7) pages.
11. Please see the suggestions for writing a better paper on my website, www .loyno.edu/~pburns.
12. You must also use either MLA Citation Style or *The Chicago Manual of Style* to cite your sources.
13. Points will be deducted if you do not follow the writing tips and the style requirements. You will lose two points for each spelling mistake and each grammar mistake.

USE THE COLLEGE'S RESOURCES

Colleges provide many resources to assist students. Writing centers, counseling offices, and librarians aid students. As I discussed earlier, the writing center improves not only your papers but also your writing ability. The counseling center aids those who need someone with whom to talk.

Research says: 70 percent of students at a major urban Southeastern university who had GPAs between 1.75 and 2.00 warned incoming freshmen to "utilize university resources for success."[6]

Table 7.3. Thoughts on How to Write Strong Papers

1. Answer the question in the introduction. Provide the answers to your questions in the first paragraph. You should write a few sentences that preview your answers. By front-loading your answers, you let the reader know that you have answered the question. Remember, the key to any paper is to answer the question.
2. Knowledge Claims. Papers are statements about knowledge claims. You need to support knowledge claims with evidence and examples. When you make a knowledge claim you need to address why government and politics works the way you claim that it does. You need to give examples of the power of the mayor in action or the ways in which the state constitution determines education policy.
3. Facts and So-What. Facts allow you to answer the question. You also want to provide greater meaning to the facts. If the federal government provides money to the states and the cities (fact), what does this tell us about the larger role of federal government in state and local government and politics (so-what)?
4. Break up long paragraphs. One goal in writing papers is to make it easy for the reader to understand your points. Therefore, you want to write three- to six-sentence paragraphs that communicate one point. Long paragraphs contain many points and they confuse the reader. Short paragraphs are more powerful because they concisely communicate one important point. You should separate different ideas and points.
5. Fewer words are better than more words. Try to eliminate unnecessary words. A good plan is to simply and concisely communicate your ideas to the reader.
6. Try not to use the word *this* when you start a sentence. Use of the word *this* alone is unclear. For example, "This shows how power works in the state." Instead, you need to explain what this is. "The federal government's control over finances shows how power works in Louisiana."
7. Try not to use quotes to stress the importance of words. Quotation marks around "words" mean so-called. For example, "the 'SAT' examines" means "the so-called SAT examines." You would be better off dropping the use of the quotation marks. The reader will still understand what you are trying to communicate.
8. *That* and *which*. In general, use *which* after a comma and use *that* when you do not use a comma. For example, "I attend Loyola University, which is a Jesuit institution."
9. Avoid proofreading mistakes at all costs!
10. Avoid the passive voice by replacing forms of to be with more active verbs.
11. *It's* and *Its*. A major difference exists between *it's* and *its*. *Its* is a modifier before a noun[7]: "The White House used *its* resources to defeat the bill." *It's* is a contraction meaning it is or it has: "*It's* easier to take Route 8 than Interstate 95." Many students believe that *it's* is a possessive, and they use the contraction incorrectly. For instance, an incorrect sentence may read, "The White House used it's resources to defeat the bill." *It's* is used incorrectly here. That sentence really says, "The White House used *it is* resources to defeat the bill." Students need to understand these differences and pay attention to detail in order to properly use *its* and *it's*.

Librarians are a first-rate resource. For example, they help students find materials for papers. At least one person exists at each college library who is waiting to assist you. Reference librarians are trained professionals who know how to find research materials. In order to properly utilize the assistance of librarians, you need to see them well in advance of your due date. Too many students wait until the last moment, but librarians need time to get information to you. In addition, like workers at writing centers, librarians neither perform miracles nor write papers. You have to do the bulk of the work, but they will help you find material.

College websites also provide excellent resources to help students. College library websites often include databases such as LexisNexis, JSTOR, and other computerized information systems. The librarians will teach you how to use these resources, which greatly facilitate composition of papers and your learning process.

Burns's Rules for Paper Writing

1. Writing takes practice
2. Avoid proofreading mistakes
3. Work in advance
4. Write drafts of your papers
5. Outlines improve clarity
6. Answer the essay question
7. Answer all parts of the essay question
8. Use evidence to support your knowledge claims
9. Make the reader understand your point

General Tip for Paper Writing

Type the assignment questions and then separate and answer each question.

NOTES

1. William Strunk Jr. and E. B. White, *The Elements of Style*, 3rd ed. (Boston: Allyn and Bacon, 2000).

2. Joseph M. Williams, *Style: The Basics of Clarity and Grace*, 7th ed. (New York: Longman, 1999).

3. For the salience of this point, I am indebted to Terri Goldson.

4. Doug Enders, "Crossing the Divide: A Survey of the High School Activities That Best Prepared Students to Write in College," *Clearing House* 75, no. 2 (2001): 62–67.

5. James Kuo, Chris Hagie, and Michael T. Miller, "Encouraging College Student Success: The Instructional Challenges, Response Strategies, and Study Skills of Contemporary Undergraduates," *Journal of Instructional Psychology* 31, no. 1 (2004): 60–67.

6. Commander and Valeri-Gold, "Ideas in Practice."

7. Definitions come from dictionary.com.

8

Notes

Write, Read, Write, Read, Read

Opinions vary regarding how to take notes. I developed my note-taking skills through trial and error, and you may have to do the same. Some argue that students should not write down everything the professor says during class. Instead, students should focus upon listening and write what they believe to be important. Others contend that students should write everything and determine later which information is important and which is not.

I support the line of thinking that students should write as much as possible during the lecture. As both a student and a professor, I found it to be quite difficult to determine importance on the fly. Selective note taking puts too much pressure on your memory. Students who try to memorize lectures often miss something important. By taking compre-hensive notes, students can determine later which parts of the lecture were important.

Students should write as much as possible during the lecture.

Taking comprehensive notes is difficult. It hurts your hand. I often got hand cramps from writing copious notes, and I see the best note tak-ers shaking their hands in pain. Taking comprehensive notes is difficult, especially when professors speak too quickly. You can ask fast-talking professors to repeat what they said. Another way to offset fast talkers is to develop a method of shorthand. You need to abbreviate words so that you can write what the professor says. Most importantly, when you adopt a method of shorthand, you need to be able to read your notes. It is important to consult your notes as soon after class as possible because you can correct your notes and understand your shorthand much better when the lecture is still fresh in your mind. When you wait to look at the notes, you often forget what you wrote or what your shorthand meant.

Others say, "Taking good notes during class is essential. Write down as much as you can, paying attention to clues about what's important. For example, teachers often write main ideas down on the board, start off a statement by saying, 'It's important,' or speak more slowly when giving facts you'll need to know."[1]

Taking good notes requires intense concentration. On many occasions, students' attention wanders during class and this daytrip, as I call it, impedes their ability to take notes. It is my view that many students regard class time as a relaxing part of their day, but in order to take notes correctly you must understand that you need to pay close attention to your professors, even the most boring ones.

Taking good notes requires intense concentration. On many occasions, students' attention wanders during class and this daytrip, as I call it, impedes their ability to take notes.

I listened to anyone who gave advice on how to take notes. I paid particular attention to professors who told the class how they studied or took notes. William H. Berentsen, a geography professor at UConn, exerted significant influence on my study skills even though I took only one course with him. Berentsen strongly encouraged students to attend class, and he explained why attendance was vital. His advice is applicable to all students, and I recommend that you try this form of note taking. Berentsen referred to many different forms of learning. Listening constituted one form. Students who heard the lecture learned more than those who missed the lecture. Writing made up a second form of learning. Students solidify their understanding of the information when they write the material.

At the end of most semesters, I see students photocopying notes in the library. If you miss class, then you need to get the notes from a classmate, preferably one of the best. You cannot rely on photocopied notes as a substitute for attending class. Notes represent one part of the class, but attendance provides context. The notes mean more when you attend class. As Berentsen noted, listening to the lecture constitutes an important form of learning, which you miss if you skip class. You cannot recover this first form of learning when you miss class.

Professor Fettweis says, "I always recommend getting notes from two people—that way, hopefully they'll be able to see what they missed."

Reading your notes makes up the third form of learning and rewriting constitutes another stage. In total, hearing, writing, reading, rewriting, and rereading notes help students understand rather than simply memorize the material. I studied for tests by working in advance and performing variations of this process.

Another key to learning that I recommend to all students is to read and recopy your notes as soon after class as possible. When I rewrote my notes as soon as I could, I understood and learned the material better than if I waited. You can also more easily identify parts of the lecture you do not understand when you recopy the notes as soon after class as possible. Even if you cannot recopy your notes immediately after a class ends, then the least you should do is reread your notes.

Although I wrote my notes only on one side of my notebook, where you take notes is a matter of personal preference. As I opened my notebook, I took notes on the page on the right and recopied the notes on the page to the left. I used the blank page to create structured notes. As

I recopied, I tried to put my notes into an outline. I used the recopying process to reflect upon the goal of the lecture and how the lecture fit into the broader picture. Oftentimes, the themes became more readily apparent as I recopied my notes because the professor would say the same thing over and over. The recopying process facilitated my attention to detail and it allowed me to anticipate exam questions. I also left lots of space between the points I wrote. Dense notes overwhelmed me.

I never tape-recorded a lecture. That does not mean you should not try it, but my advice is to be cautious about tape-recording lectures. If you are going to tape, you need to receive your professors' permission. Tape-recorded lectures should only be used to clarify parts of your notes that you do not understand. They are a complement to, but not a substitute for, note taking. Even if you decide to tape, you still need to take notes. Unfortunately, the few students who have tape-recorded my lectures just sat there and listened to what I said.

The use of computers to take notes in class is a recent phenomenon. I type faster than I write. Consequently, I took notes by writing and by typing in order to determine which method works best for me, and I suggest you do the same.

Note taking by computer presents a special set of distractions. The Internet and solitaire will tempt students who use the computer to take notes. Recently, I saw one of my students playing solitaire on his laptop during my lecture. A few days later, I watched a professor lecture to a class on C-SPAN, and as the camera pulled back, I could see at least one student playing solitaire on his computer. As is the case with handwriting your notes, you need to remain focused in order to maximize the information you collect in class.

When I was an undergraduate, my uncle Tom and my grandfather came to UConn for a basketball game on a Tuesday night. We ate on campus, and my uncle asked whether I would attend the game. I told him I had class and he asked whether missing one class would make that big a difference. At first glance, it appears that one absence is no big deal, but I offered the following explanations for going to class. First, the class met one time per week, so one absence equaled a week's worth of absences. Second, I did not want to miss that form of learning. I learned so much in class and skipping would set me back. Third, I may need to miss a future class for a legitimate reason, such as illness.

I have reflected upon my uncle's question over the years. Would it really have mattered if I missed one class? Missing one class makes a difference for all the reasons I listed above, and because regular attendance and studying established a rhythm and pattern that made it easier for me to navigate the semester. Missing a class needlessly disrupted my flow.

Burns's Rules on Note Taking

1. Reread your notes as soon after class as possible

2. Recopy your notes

3. If you miss class, then get the notes from at least one classmate, preferably a good student

---

General Tips on Note Taking

1. Write as much as possible during the lecture
2. Write your notes on one side of the notebook and recopy them to the other side

---

NOTE

1. Melissa Ezarik, "Be a Real SURVIVOR," *Career World* 30, no. 2 (2001): 6–10.

Your Professors

Is the Professor Dr. Jekyll or Mr./Ms. Hyde?

CREATE A LEARNING PARTNERSHIP

A student-professor partnership facilitates learning. Your professors cannot teach you if you do not want to learn. As a professor, one of my greatest frustrations is that I cannot get all students to care about learning. As I said before, you must care in order to learn. You cannot learn if your professors do not teach. Hopefully, you will not experience this phenomenon during your college career.

Research says: 30 percent of students at a major urban Southeastern university who had GPAs between 1.75 and 2.00 warned incoming freshmen to "get to know your professors."[1]

You should create a learning partnership with your professors. My suggestion is to visit your professors' office hours on a regular basis. Universities and colleges require professors to hold office hours. Office hours are not a time for you to simply chat with your professor, although that may happen. I like to find out something about my students and their backgrounds, but not all professors are this way. Office hours are a time for you to ask questions about the lectures and books. They provide a venue for you to determine how much of the class you understand. You can use these visits to ask them important questions about exams, papers, and your performance.

Others say, "Frequent student-faculty contact can enhance students' motivation, involvement, and intellectual commitment, encouraging them to think about their own values and future plans."[2]

Your professors will be impressed that you cared enough to visit them. Office hours allow your professors to get to know you. Many students have no one to write their letters of recommendation for law school, medical school, or other graduate schools because no professors know them. If they had visited office hours and created relationships with their professors, then they would not have this problem.

Others say, "It is the quality of the [student] contact [with professors], not the quantity that matters."[3]

Students who only visit office hours either directly before or especially right after an exam give the impression that they care about the grade rather than learning. If you visit your professor once a month during the semester, you give the impression that you care about learning and grades. I suggest seeing your professors early in the semester. A visit within the first two or three weeks of the semester allows students and professors to know each other better, and it provides students with greater insight into the course.

Professors understand that you care about your grades. When I was in graduate school, I received an unsatisfactory grade on a paper and I asked the professor how I could improve. The professor asked whether my grade was the real issue. Initially, I said no, but then I said yes. I told him that my grades were important to me. I think he graded students lower on the first paper to see how we would respond. I wanted to improve so that I could learn *and* earn better grades.

Others say, "Students [should] go see the professors during their office hours: this shows genuine concern for their achievement, begins to connect the student and the institution AND begins to help the professors see the student as an individual . . . and assess how much the student has already learned in the course."[4]

Relationship building with professors adds positive pressure to students. Students who build relationships with their professors have incentives to perform well because they will want to maintain their reputations as good students. I felt this way when I created bonds with my professors, and many of the students who develop a professional relationship with me work extra hard to perform well in my courses. In fact, on more than one occasion, students who built relationships with me have apologized for poor preferences and vowed to improve. To the best of my memory, these students delivered on these promises.

In line with building partnerships with your professors, as a common courtesy, you should let your professors know in advance that you will not be in class. If you cannot provide this information before you miss a class, then you should contact your professor as soon as possible to give him or her the general reason for your absence. Advance notice of absences lets professors know that you missed for a reason. If you don't tell professors why you missed, then they may assume that you were sleeping or doing some other irresponsible activity. However, I have had students who missed several classes and provided an excuse each time. After the second miss, the excuses become less credible. Therefore, make sure that your reasons for missing class are valid and try your best to limit the number of times you must miss a class.

PAY ATTENTION

You must listen to professors because they make up the tests, grade the papers, design the course, and run the class. Many students do not pay attention to their professors. I took an introductory course at UConn with Skip Lowe, one of the best professors I ever had. I use him as model for some of my lecturing strategies. Lowe told a class of about 200 students that they should come to see him if they wanted to know how to take notes from the book. I was the only student who sought this advice. Lowe congratulated me for coming to his office.

Before the teaching assistants posted the exam grades, Lowe explained that the students had performed poorly on the exam. Then he pointed to me. I sat in the first row of the second section in a large lecture hall. I pointed to myself, and he said, "Yes . . . you! What did you score on the exam?" I said I did not know and he told me I received a 96, the highest grade in the class. He explained that I was the only student who cared enough to find out how I should study. More importantly, I took Lowe's advice and followed his instructions for studying from the book.

Before the teaching assistants posted the exam grades, the professor explained that the students performed poorly on the exams. Then, he pointed to me. I sat in the first row of the second section in a large lecture hall. I pointed to myself, and he said, "Yes . . . you! What did you score on the exam?" I said I did not know, and he told me I received a 96, the highest grade in the class. He explained that I was the only student who cared enough to find out how I should study. More importantly, I took the professor's advice and followed his instructions for studying from the book.

Professor Fettweis asks, "Did the rest of the class beat the hell out of you in the hallway afterward?"

Burns responds, "No, I really do not think my classmates cared."

In my freshmen year, I took an introductory writing course. For our first paper, Professor Dougherty told the class that we must follow the outline presented in the book. He was adamant. I remember studying that outline. My paper mirrored this outline. When Dougherty returned the papers, he said that all but one were bad. He explained that only one student followed his explicit instructions. Then he read the paper. It was mine. These events reinforced my attitude that I needed to pay attention to the professor.

In less than two years, I went from receiving D's in accounting and getting tossed out of the guidance counselor's office in high school to earning the highest grades in college courses and receiving public praise from my professors. Part of my success stemmed from being the *only* student who listened to my professors.

One of the keys to my academic success is that I am an excellent advice taker. I seek and implement advice. As a professor, I notice that many students pay little attention to the things I say. During one semester, a student wrote a rough draft, which I read. The paper needed significant revisions. I gave explicit instructions about how to improve the paper. The student did not follow my advice. She simply made proofreading corrections. She asked me why she received a less than average grade on her final draft. I explained that she did not take my advice. The student did an excellent job of writing a draft and receiving advice but she did not incorporate my feedback into her final work.

KNOW YOUR PROFESSORS
No two professors are the same. Each professor values different things. You need to know with whom you are dealing so you can give professors what they want. For instance, Fred Kort, a political science professor and legend at UConn, valued attendance. He based a good portion of his grade on attendance. Therefore, I made sure to never— and I mean never—miss his class. Kort also despised it when students left class early. I made sure to never leave his class early. My Introduction to American Government professor stressed the importance of the assigned readings. I made sure that I knew those readings as best I could.

As a professor, I value many things, including attendance and well-written papers without proofreading mistakes. I stress these things in class, and the best students pay attention to what I say. At the beginning of the semester, I inform students both verbally and via the syllabus that they will receive a good grade if they read, take notes, come to all classes, and complete their assignments in advance. When professors make these kinds of guarantees, you should do as they say.

Your professors try to instill values in you. Kort attempted to get students to understand the importance of always attending class. My first-year political science professor communicated the value of reading comprehension. Conrad Raabe, my colleague in political science at Loyola University New Orleans, requires students to read the *New York Times* on a daily basis. Conrad instills the importance of being informed, and he develops students' ability to apply theoretical concepts to real-world events.

Professors try to instill values in you.

I made it a point to ask my friends and classmates about professors' reputations (for more on developing a kitchen cabinet, see chapter 10). I wanted to know which professors were hard, unreasonable, easy, interesting, or challenging. I also asked about the professors' policies and standards. For the most part, I did not take a course without having a strong understanding of the professor with whom I was dealing.

Colleges and universities promote small class sizes. At UConn, enrollment exceeded 100 in some of my classes. I made the class size smaller by attending every class and sitting up front. Many of my classmates did not attend class on a regular basis and therefore I benefited from smaller class size. I created a one-on-one relationship with my professors by attending class and visiting office hours, and you can do the same.

Shrink the class size by attending all classes and sitting in the front.

DO NOT MISTAKE KINDNESS FOR WEAKNESS

In the TV show *Cops*, after police officers let people go without a ticket, I often hear them say, "Do not mistake my kindness for weakness." You should not mistake professors' kindness, outgoing personality, or age for weakness. Simply because professors are friendly, outgoing, or young does not mean they are easy! Some of the most demanding professors I took were also some of the nicest and most easygoing. Professors are not your friends, even though they may seem like they are. No matter what, professors are still in charge and you must prepare and work hard.

Simply because professors are friendly, outgoing, or young does not mean they are easy!

To learn and to score well on exams, it is important to know the criteria professors use to grade exams or papers. Ask your professors which kinds of information or detail they want on exams and papers. In office hours or in class, you can ask professors about what they regard as quality answers and essays. Pay attention to what professors say in class and on their syllabi. In class, I tell students that they need to use examples from the book to support their claims. The best students write this comment in their notes and they make sure to provide examples from the book. In my syllabus, I spell out the grading criteria for papers and exams (see the American Government syllabus in chapter 3). The best students understand the criteria, which they consult when they write their papers.

FETTWEIS'S FIVE STAGES OF GRIEF

Stage 1: Shock

As a student and as a professor, I have experienced the five stages of grief after receiving a poor grade. Shock is stage one. When students open up the blue book or paper and see a 40 or an F, they experience a chill or tingling feeling.[5] Many ask, "Is this score based on a 100-point scale?"

Professor Fettweis's Five Stages of Grief after Receiving a Poor Grade, and Student Responses at Each Stage

1. Shock: "No way!" "I can't believe it!"

2. Anger: "That damn professor!"

3. Bargaining: "I know you say A is the answer but couldn't B also be correct?" "Can I get partial credit?" "Considering I didn't have enough time, can you drop the grade for the lowest essay?" "Can I do makeup work?"

4. Depression: "Why am I even in college?" "I should drop this class."

5. Acceptance: "Well, maybe I can do it better next time." "Maybe I should study next time."

Stage 2: Anger

The shock stage lasts briefly and it transitions quickly to stage 2, anger: "How could this bastard professor do this to me?" On many occasions, students look at their grade and immediately ask how they received this grade. These students are emotional and have not even looked at the professor's comments. You should take the exam back to your room and think about it for a few days. I ask students to come back after reflecting on the exam because they are volatile in the anger phase. They often say incredibly rude things to me when they are in this stage.

Like most professors, I put great thought into the grades I give and I make extensive comments on students' tests and papers. I read through the papers and my comments at least twice before I assign a final grade. I resent it when students see the grade and ask me *immediately* how they received their mark—without even reading my comments.

The anger phase can last forever. I am still angry over receiving a certain grade in graduate school. If I had confronted the professor immediately, I would have made some very inappropriate comments.

Considering the fact that I now interact with this professor on a professional level, this anger would have translated into a poor career decision.

You should wait to ask your professor about your grade. You need to make sure you are out of the anger stage. You need to determine why the professor assigned this grade. Which kinds of comments did the professor make? Was the professor correct? Did you provide an answer that the professor may have missed? Could you have been clearer?

Stage 3: Bargaining

When many students ask about a grade, they attempt to bargain with their professor. Please avoid the bargaining stage. One form of bargaining occurs when students try to defend incorrect answers: "Can't B be correct for question 3, also? Can't I get partial credit?"[6]

You must not tell professors you should have received a better grade because you are an A student or because you never received a low grade in the past. GPAs and prior grades are irrelevant. All that matters is whether you accurately answered the questions. If GPA and previous grades determined future grades, then you really should not have to show up to class. When students tell me that they have never received a C, I hear them telling me that I am stupid. They are really saying that my judgment is incorrect and everyone else's is right. You should avoid this kind of language and confrontation.

"I had one student tell me, 'I knew the answer; I just didn't write it down. Can I get some points for that?'"
—Dr. Matthew O. Thomas

You should not ask professors to change your grade because you are going to lose your scholarship or your parents will not let you return to school. Please. One bargainer wanted to drop my course *after* she completed *all* of the course work for the semester. Another asked if I could raise his grade above a D because his father would not let him return to school after he received such low grades. Clearly, this student thought that bargaining, rather than merit and the criteria laid out in the syllabus, determined the final grades.

Students who make such bargains tend to miss class and turn in incomplete assignments, and are not interested in doing well. You need to be mature enough to do all the hard work necessary for the class or suffer the consequences. In my experience, on most occasions, you will receive the grades you deserve. Sometimes you will work really hard and get a C, whereas under certain conditions you will receive an A without working very hard, but these are exceptions rather than the rule.

Students also drive me insane when they lobby for grades. Lobbying is a form of bargaining. A number of students tell me over and over that they need an A in my class. This information is irrelevant. Student performance on graded materials is the factor I consider when I assign grades.

Another form of bargaining and lobbying takes place when students *tell me* how smart they are. More than one student came up to me after the first American Government class to tell me that they took an advanced placement (AP) government course and they know everything. One student who made such a proclamation barely passed and another would have failed had she not dropped the course. Do not *tell* your professors how smart you are. Instead, *show* your professors how smart you are.

Stages 4 and 5: Depression and Acceptance

Depression and acceptance mark the final stages. In the depression phase, students become really disappointed over their grades. I was really angry with myself for receiving a C-plus in Oceanography.[7] Depression replaced anger. I stewed over the grade and questioned how I could let an elective drag my GPA down. Eventually, I learned from this experience and accepted my grade. In the long run, the class provided more positives than negatives. Some students reach acceptance much quicker than others.

Many professors understand the stages of grief partly because they face rejection on a regular basis. As scholars, a great deal of professors' research is rejected and heavily criticized by our peers. The *American Political Science Review (APSR)*, the top journal in my field, rejects 88 percent of the manuscripts it receives annually.[8] In the words of the *APSR*'s editor, "I spent a great deal of my time conveying bad news to authors."[9]

My work has received some highly critical and deeply personal comments. Regarding one of my works, a reviewer remarked, "What there is is tortuously formulated, clumsily analyzed, and . . . wretchedly written. The study's main thesis is important and compelling but obtusely presented and not original." I had to convince myself to get to the acceptance stage as quickly as possible. I needed to cull the most useful information from these reviews in order to rewrite my paper. Eventually, I made the necessary changes and this work was accepted. When you receive poor or unsatisfactory grades, often the best you can do is to figure out what went wrong and try to correct those mistakes in the future.

If after reflection you decide the professor was wrong, you need to be crystal clear about which mistakes you believe the professor made. You need to show the professor why your answer was correct. You should listen intently to the professor and not take anything that he or she says personally. When you talk to the professor, you must remain professional. Many times students say awful things to professors when they protest grades. You need to focus upon why your grade should be better. You need to provide evidence.

Research says, "College students had a poorly defined sense of how prepared they were for a test or how well they had done on a test once they had taken it."[10]

Professors make mistakes, and some even admit it. Few professors, if any, will listen to students during the shock or anger stages. Would you change someone's grade if that student insulted you? The only time I remember switching a grade occurred when a student came to my office about one week after I returned the papers. The student had received a B. She showed me her paper and asked how she received her grade when I wrote *good* and *great* all over it. I looked at the paper and the student was correct. I had provided no basis for a B. She deserved an A, which she received.

In my college career, which spanned three presidential administrations, I questioned only one grade. To this day, I feel that the professor assigned the grade in an arbitrary fashion. You must be very careful when you question professors about your grade. Here are some pieces of advice on asking why you received a grade.

Several weeks after receiving a grade I felt I did not deserve, I went to talk to the professor. I literally thought the professor made a mistake when he calculated my grade. Two students named Burns took the course, and I thought the professor mistook me for the other Burns. I did not bargain at all. I simply asked how I received my grade. He explained the grades on the final paper, exam, and class participation. After listening to him, I thought there was nothing I could do, I thanked him for his time, and I left.

Some professors assign grades in an arbitrary fashion. They may not be able to explain why you received a particular grade. If this is the case, you should talk to the chair of the department or the dean's office to find out the formal process for appealing a grade. At all times, I strongly advise you to be professional and unemotional.

Burns's Rules for Dealing with Professors

1. Attend office hours on a regular basis
2. Listen to your professors
3. Follow your professors' advice
4. Understand the criteria your professors use to grade exams and papers
5. Understand the five stages of grief you may experience when you receive a less than satisfactory grade

---

General Tip for Dealing with Professors

Create a learning partnership with your professors

NOTES

1. Commander and Valeri-Gold, "Ideas in Practice."

2. Maureen E. Wilson, "Teaching, Learning, and Millennial Students," *New Directions for Student Services* 106 (Summer 2004): 59–71.

3. Wilson, "Teaching, Learning, and Millennial Students."

4. Paul Vermette, "Improving Understanding and Increasing Grades: 4 Tips for a Fall Freshman at Columbus Day, an Open Letter to My Son at College," *College Student Journal* 34, no. 4 (2000): 611–15.

5. According to dictionary.com, a blue book is "a blank notebook with blue covers in which to write the answers to examination questions."

6. For this information, I am indebted to Christopher J. Fettweis.

7. My college roommate recommended this class. He still cannot believe that I could not calculate Fahrenheit into Celsius.

8. Lee Sigelman, "Report of the Editor of the *American Political Science Review,* 2002–2003," *PS: Political Science and Politics* 37 (2004): 139–42.

9. Sigelman, "Report of the Editor of the *American Political Science Review,*" p. 141.

10. Stephen T. Peverly, Karen E. Brobst, Mark Graham, and Ray Shaw, "College Adults Are Not Good at Self-Regulation: A Study on the Relationship of Self-Regulation, Note Taking, and Test Taking," *Journal of Educational Psychology* 95, no. 2 (2003): 335–46.

10

Scheduling of Classes
Make a Well-Balanced Schedule

If your school generates a schedule for you prior to your first year, you should strongly consider changing that schedule. This first schedule is impersonal. It does not take your academic strengths and weaknesses into account. This schedule may also provide as many as five demanding courses that you do not need to take in the first semester.

In every semester, and especially the first one, I advise you to take a well-balanced schedule. A balanced schedule includes two classes that you need to take in order to fulfill college requirements, two major requirements, and one general elective, which is a course in any subject. If you create a schedule that gets all requirements out of the way in one semester, then you will forget why you are in college. College becomes even more difficult when you do not take at least one class you want to take.

A balanced schedule also consists of a combination of challenging courses, moderately difficult courses, and easier courses. Challenging courses consist of those in subjects you find particularly difficult. In my case, for example, I found math to be quite challenging but I really liked classes on government, politics, history, and sociology. When I took a required math course, I also enrolled in two classes that I wanted to take.

Students should understand which professors are challenging and which are not. Other students provide great insight into which professors and courses to take. Their advice will help you make a more informed decision. In some instances, students will advise you to take an easy course or a professor who is not especially challenging. Students also recommend challenging professors who inspire them. At Loyola University, many students tell others to take courses taught by Michael A. Ross in the History Department. Mike is far from easy. Students tell me he is downright demanding. His classes are full because he engages and challenges students. When I was a student, I took Skip Lowe's course even though my friend told me the class was hard.

CREATE A KITCHEN CABINET

President Andrew Jackson received counsel from his so-called kitchen cabinet, an informal group of advisers, most of whom were his friends. Jackson relied on this group because he could not trust the members of his official cabinet. While I believe you can trust your official advisers, I think you should also use a kitchen cabinet.

Research says: 32 percent of students at a major urban Southeastern university who had GPAs between 1.75 and 2.00 warned incoming freshmen to "rely on friends and family for support."[1]

My kitchen cabinet served me well during my college years. My friend Kiley taught me that pitfalls remain even after a strong first year. My sister advised me to take a mix of courses and she also counseled me on the importance of my first year. My friend Frank stressed the value of hard work. Tom, my college roommate, and I told each other which courses to take and which not to take. Thankfully for both of us, Tom told me about Amii Omara-Otunnu and I encouraged Tom to take classes with the great Edgar Litt. Overall, you should know what you are getting into before you take classes, and a kitchen cabinet helps in this regard.

ORDER

Many students think they must take required courses in a certain order. In some cases this is true. For example, students cannot take an advanced course in psychology without first taking Introduction to Psychology. In many instances, however, students do not have to take classes in any order. As I often tell students, they do not need to fulfill most of their requirements in any order, they only need to complete the required courses by the time they finish. This advice is important because some students needlessly overload on required courses at the beginning of their college career. This overload prevents students from taking a balanced schedule.

COURSE LOAD

I recommend that you take four courses in your first semester and that you take no more than five classes in any one semester. Taking four courses in your first semester is a wise strategy because it provides you with more time to adjust to college life. Students can make up the three credit hours rather easily during the next three and one-half years, and in some schools, taking four classes will not put students behind at all. At many colleges, students take five courses per semester. A schedule with six classes puts unnecessary stress on students. It requires too much of students, who often do not learn as much as possible because they must cut studying short in one class to prepare for another.

BEWARE THE COURSE CATALOG

The course catalog provides short summaries of all the courses. It can deceive. Some descriptions look quite appealing but the course does not live up the promise. When I first went to college, I thought courses on Star Trek, music, sports, and comic books would be easy and fun, but I was wrong. You need to find out more details about these courses before you enroll. Summaries may not capture the strengths of interesting courses. My advice is to make certain that you understand who the professor is and the difficulty and content of any course before you enroll.

Burns's Rules for Scheduling

1. Take a well-balanced schedule every semester
2. Get advice from others about which classes to take
3. Do not take classes simply to get requirements out of the way
4. Beware the descriptions in the course catalog

General Tip for Scheduling

Change the first schedule you receive and tailor it to your preferences

---

NOTE

1. Commander and Valeri-Gold, "Ideas in Practice."

In-Class Etiquette

Oh, Behave!

Attendance is always mandatory. I do not care if the professor does not include attendance as part of the grade or if the syllabus allows three un-excused absences. You must attend all classes. If you are going to miss class for some legitimate reason, you should let the professor know in advance. I understand that people get sick and certain emergencies arise. When these things occur you need to let the professor know in a timely fashion. I believe strongly that learning diminishes if you do not attend class.

Once in class, you must understand that class time is quite serious. Lectures and class time are difficult. Too many students just sit there and listen as the professor gives a lecture. You need to take copious notes (see chapter 8 for more on note taking). Most people can neither memorize lectures nor determine what is important as the professor talks. Therefore, you must rely on your notes.

Don't talk to others during class, period!

Where should you sit? Many people suggest that you should sit up front, but not necessarily in the first row. Sitting in the front section is a good plan because students in the front are closest to the professor and are most likely to be engaged by the professor. The best students do not always sit in the front. Some of my better students sit in the back, and a number of students who do not perform well sit in the first row. If I were to generalize, I would say that the better students tend to sit toward the front and those who are less engaged usually sit in the back. My experience has been that the biggest troublemakers sit in the very last row.

"I liked the back row. It allowed me to experience the class in its entirety."
                    —Dr. Matthew O. Thomas, graduated magna cum laude

---

Speaking of trouble, you need to respect classmates and professors. A number of students lash out at their classmates during discussion. This action is quite distasteful. Students have also reacted harshly to me. You can challenge a professor, but you need to be respectful. You should respond in an unemotional manner. Most students think that class is debate time. Instead, class time is about learning. I think you should contribute to class discussions if you can add something substantive. By contrast, if you are talking just to debate and be heard, then I suggest you save your breath and everyone else's time.

"Over the years I had sensed that student misbehavior was on the rise: rudeness, lateness, loudness, distractedness, and the myriad small sins that irritate teachers. It was not as if these young louts were protesting a war or engaging in civil disobedience; they were just plain rude."[1]
                    —college professor on student behavior

DISCUSSION

In my view, many students do not know how to participate in class discussions. When I was in graduate school, I lost points for the class participation grade in one course because I talked too much in general. The professor never laid out his expectations for the class participation grade, but he provided excellent feedback when I asked about my grade. He told me I talked too much. I know this sounds strange, and it shocked me, but he was right. When professors grade class participation, they encourage unlimited talking by some students. On many occasions, I talked simply to say something. I did not contribute to the class discussion. When you talk in class, you must add something to the class discussion. Before you talk in class, imagine you are writing instead of speaking. Is what you are about to say actually bringing up relevant points? Are you moving the discussion forward? Are you adding something?

Others say, "What happened to civility? Has being rude become socially acceptable? Is abuse becoming commonplace?" Colleges and universities, instructors, and even students are increasingly frustrated by a variety of negative campus behaviors. They impact life on campus for everyone, in and out of the classroom. Consider the following concerns:

- verbal abuse by students
- assaults in the classroom
- confrontations in the hallways
- inappropriate classroom language and responses
- students entering class late and loudly
- skipping classes
- preparing to leave early from the classroom
- loud gum chewing
- speaking out of turn
- cell phones and pagers going off and being answered
- inappropriate classroom attire
- side conversations during instruction
- students reading the newspaper
- doing e-mail or surfing the web
- video games on computers and cell phones
- student-to-student hostility.[2]

You should not ramble on when you speak in class. Instead, you should make your point and stop talking. Too many students just talk and talk without saying anything. You want to avoid doing this.

Approach talking in class much the same way you would a limited-minute cell phone plan: be strategic about how long you talk and when.

I understand that public speaking frightens many people. In my first years as a professor, I called on students at random. I stopped this tactic because most students complained vehemently about it and many students literally got upset when I called on them. At least one student cried when I called on her. I have some suggestions for the nontalkers. First, if you want or need to talk in class, then you should consult with your professor about the best way to accomplish this goal. Second, you may want to write out what you going to say before you talk. It is good advice to write out what you have to say before you talk even if you are confident. By writing out what you want to say, you can make sure that your points add something or move the discussion forward.

Professor Fettweis says, "Students have to learn to debate without getting personal—and without taking things too personally."

Finally, for those of you who do not talk much or at all in class, please do not be fooled by the talkers. In my courses, the nontalkers are some of the best students in the class. Unfortunately, they believe that the talkers know more than they do and are smarter than they are. This assumption is incorrect. Those who talk the most are not always the smartest or the most informed. They are just the ones who are most comfortable talking. By contrast, the nontalkers may be quite smart and informed, but they are the least comfortable talking.

Professor Fettweis says, "I was just advising a student on how to contribute in class. He was a nervous type—I advised him to know exactly what he was going to say before he spoke. The mind tends to blank when all eyes are on you . . . and then panic sets in quickly, and paralysis follows."

Burns's Rules for In-Class Behavior

1. Understand that class time is quite serious
2. Pay attention
3. Take copious notes
4. Behave
5. Respect the professor
6. Respect the other students
7. Avoid sidebar conversations
8. Do not pass notes
9. Add something substantive to the discussion when you speak
10. Talkers do not necessarily know more than nontalkers

General Tips for In-Class Behavior

1. Sit up front

2. Nontalkers should write out what they want to say before they speak

NOTES

1. David D. Perlmutter, "What Works When Students and Teachers Both Misbehave," *Education Digest* 70, no. 1 (2004): 48–52.

2. "Controlling Inappropriate Classroom Behavior," *Perspective* 19, no. 10 (2004): 3–4.

12

Evaluate Your Performance

Figure Out What You Did Wrong and Try to Fix It

I once heard Bill Belichick, head coach of three teams that won the Super Bowl, say that true champions figure out what went wrong, and they put a plan in place to try to correct those mistakes. I encourage students to follow Belichick's advice.

You will almost certainly experience low moments in the classroom during your college career. When you receive low grades or you do not perform as well as you would have liked, you need to assess why you underperformed. You need to ask, "Why did I receive this grade? What went wrong?"

The questions in the following paragraphs enable you to determine what went wrong. How much did you study for this paper or test? Did you dedicate enough time? I ask students who receive poor grades how much time they spent on the paper or test. Most often, time is the major factor that affects grades. Students do not spend enough time studying for an exam, and their test scores reflect this lack of preparation. A student and I discussed once why she received a 78 on an American Government exam. She told me she started to study at noon the day before the test. I told her she did extraordinarily well considering that she started to study for the test about nineteen hours before the exam began.

I do not think two or three days enables you to adequately prepare for a test, so less than one day is certainly too little.

I do not have a magic formula for how long you should study for an exam. You will have to determine the time that is proper for you. At least two weeks of preparation served me well. I prepared for about an hour or two a day for tests. I read my notes, outlined the book, and then tried to commit each to memory over this time.

It is neither necessary nor helpful to study directly before a test. Many of my better students do not study in the hallways or the classroom immediately prior to an exam. They study well enough in advance so that all they need to do is take the test. Many other students consult their notes right up to the point where they professor passes out the exam. As a student, I found this action to be confusing and stressful. If you prepare in advance, then you need only review the material the night before the test. In general, I walked into the classroom right before the exam started because I did not want my classmates to confuse me or stress me out as they quizzed each other about the test. This last-minute cram session only illustrates that students have prepared inadequately for the test.

Did you study the wrong material? Which kinds of questions did you answer incorrectly? By paying attention to these kinds of questions, you can allot more time to these areas on the next exam. Sometimes I scored poorly on a test because I concentrated on the notes and the professor focused upon the readings, or vice versa. You should analyze your tests after you receive your grade. Each professor is different and consequently each creates exams in a somewhat unique manner.

Which kinds of comments did the professor make on your test or paper? I understand that not all professors make extensive comments on exams, but many do. I provide many suggestions to my students. I am convinced that many students do not read these comments. They look at the grade and put the test away. You cannot improve if you do not know what you did wrong. I think some students have the attitude that the professor is just mean or does not like them, and that is why they re-

ceived a particular grade. You will never improve if you hold this attitude. Recently, I gave an exam back to a student who looked at the grade
and immediately said, "How do I get an A on the exam?" My answer was
simple: "Answer the questions correctly." The student received B's on
both exams and I do not think she assessed how she could improve. You
should ask professors how to improve your exams or papers. In order to
accomplish this goal, you need to bring your exam or paper to the professor and be prepared to answer some of the aforementioned questions.

I provide many suggestions to my students.

I am convinced that many students do not read these comments.

Did you overstudy? Sometimes, a particular course psyches out students. So much hype surrounds certain courses that students panic and
overstudy for these tests. This happened to me in a couple of my undergraduate courses. Other students confused me and increased my stress
level, so to avoid getting psyched out, I studied alone. For me, studying
was an individualistic pursuit.

I often found study groups to be ineffective. Group sessions helped me
only when I did not understand the material. Typically, two distinct groups
come together to study. The larger group consists of those who neither
work hard nor attend class regularly. The hardworking students make up
the second group. The latter group usually helps the former group. Consequently, I found this exercise to be futile for the one who worked hard. At
some point during your studying, you may want to select one or two other
hardworking students and have a chat about the exam, but for the most
part, studying is a difficult and individualistic enterprise.

Others find that group activities benefit all students. One of my colleagues claimed that he learned the material better by teaching others in
group sessions. Therefore, you may want to experiment with group sessions and see how they work for you.

Do not be misled by your study group. On a number of occasions,
students have defended an incorrect response by stating, "That's the

answer our group agreed upon." You cannot rely on the group to find the answer for you. You must find the correct response for yourself. If you have doubts about a particular topic, then I suggest you ask the professor for clarification. You need to work in advance, however, in order to receive this clarification. You cannot ask for explanations of topics if you start to study the night before the exam.

Do not obsess over the exam. In many of the more challenging courses, I obsessed over certain exams and thought about the course at all times, as if this stress helped me. Instead, you should create a long-range study plan and execute it. Prepare on a consistent basis and make sure you understand the material that will be covered on the test. If this course is the most difficult one you will take in a semester, then give it proper attention. You may want to prepare a little bit each day, but do not overdo it as the exam approaches. Finally, do not believe the hype until you take the test, and then assess your preparation and performance.

Once you have determined what went wrong, you need to fix your deficiencies and assess whether your modifications worked. Unfortunately, sometimes you will prepare and study hard for a test, paper, or even a course and you will not receive a good grade. My experiences suggest that this is a rare occurrence. When you study hard but perform poorly, it is all right to be disappointed, but you should not be upset. Sometimes a C is the best you can do. In undergraduate work I received a C-plus in two courses: Oceanography and Introduction to Philosophy, and these grades were certainly the best I could have achieved. I did not understand these subjects no matter how hard I tried. The real tragedy happens when you receive low grades because you did not try. As Belichick noted, you must recognize your mistakes and try to correct them. If you continue to try to fix your mistakes, then you will improve.

Burns's Rules for Evaluating Your Performance

1. Assess why you underperformed
2. Determine why you succeeded
3. Ask professors how you can improve

General Tips for Evaluating Your Performance

1. Do not obsess over exams
2. Determine whether groups or individualistic studying works best for you

Good Student versus Not-So-Good Student

Which One Are You?
Which One Will You Be?

At the conclusion of one final-exam period, I returned term papers to the students. One student, whom I shall refer to as Fred, had given me trouble all semester. Fred looked at the grade, which was a D-minus, and then asked what the grade meant. I do not discuss grades with students as soon as I return papers because I do not want to deal with students who are in the anger stage. Fred asked about his final grade in the course even though I had yet to grade his final exam. A few minutes later, as other students were still taking their tests, Fred returned and asked to see me in the hallway. He wanted to discuss the paper grade, and I explained that I would not talk about anyone's paper grades for at least a few days. I declined the request and, a day later when Fred had reached the acceptance stage, he e-mailed to apologize for pressing me about grades.

After this encounter, I looked at the students who were still taking the exam and focused upon the best students in the class. At that point, I decided to compare Fred to those I regarded as the best in the class. I took out my yellow notepad, drew a line down the center, and wrote "good student" on one side and "Fred" on the other. I compared these students to provide an indication of the typical performance of good and bad students.

ATTENDANCE

In my opinion, the best students are chronically in class. Good students rarely miss class, and when they do, they usually have excellent reasons. Many good students attained perfect attendance for this 8 A.M. class. Fred attended irregularly. Some weeks Fred showed up to one class, other weeks he missed both classes, but he rarely made both classes in the same week. Fred offered many excuses for absences. One week he was sick, the next week Fred needed to go off campus for a school-affiliated event, and the next week he was sick again. Irregular attendance is a major warning sign that you are not performing at your maximum.

"Don't cry wolf. You will really be sick at some point during the semester so save your absences."

—Dr. Matthew O. Thomas

SPECIAL TREATMENT

The best students tend not to ask for special treatment. For instance, they do not ask for extensions of deadlines. By contrast, not-so-good students often try to cut special deals. They want to postpone exam dates and extend deadlines for papers. The avalanche often traps them and they need extra time for some other test or project. Frequently, I deny student requests for extensions of deadlines because I find that extra time only delays procrastination and all-night studying. Students infrequently use extensions to spend extra time on their assignments. Normally, the good students do not need an extension because they already work ahead (see Table 13.1).

Table 13.1.   Good Student versus Not-So-Good Student

Good Students	Not-So-Good Students
Attend every class	Attend class on an irregular basis
Study on a regular basis	Study on an irregular basis
Need no special treatment	Ask for special treatment, such as paper extensions
View grades as their responsibility	View grades as someone or something else's responsibility and fault
Pay attention to detail	Make careless mistakes
Take advantage of extra-credit opportunities	Do not take advantage of extra-credit assignments
View grades as impersonal	View grades as personal
College is their priority	College is one part of a full plate

OPPORTUNITIES TO IMPROVE GRADES AND TO LEARN

During the semester, I offer many extra-credit opportunities, most of which include attending a lecture and writing a one-page summary about the significance of the talk. I also give points to students who look up answers to interesting questions that arise in class. These extra-credit assignments are learning opportunities. For the most part, the best students complete all extra-credit assignments. They take advantage of these opportunities even when their grades are extremely high.

The Paradox[1]

The students who get extra credit do not need it

The students who need it do not complete the extra-credit assignments

---

In general, the not-so-good students do not take advantage of extra-credit opportunities. If they complete these assignments at all, they usually do so at the very end of the semester when they fear they will fail the course. At the end of most semesters, students in jeopardy of failing ask me how they can improve their grades. That question always blows me away because I offer so many extra-credit points during the semester.

SEEKING ASSISTANCE

Many students, regardless of their grades, do not seek the assistance of their professors. Those students who ask me for help tend to be the very best in my class. They usually have a strong desire to improve. The not-so-good students rarely come for help. Fred visited my office hours after failing the first test. I told him to attend class regularly and read and consult with me in order to improve. Fred did not follow my advice.

WHOSE RESPONSIBILITY IS IT?

Most of the best students believe it is up to them to determine their grade. They believe that their professors grade in an impersonal fashion. They view their grade as the outcome of what they learn and how hard they work rather than how the professor feels about them. By contrast, the not-so-good students think they lost a popularity contest. They believe their grade is not a reflection of their effort and knowledge. Instead, the not-so-good students think their grade reflects how the professor feels about them. They regard grades as something personal between their professors and them. For the most part, grades are impersonal. If you believe that your grade is a by-product of how the teacher feels about you, then you will never improve. Why should you? Your grade was only the result of how the professor felt about you. The best students place the onus upon themselves and try to improve regardless of their GPA.

When I was a college student, I felt my grades were my responsibility. I firmly believed my hard work and dedication determined my grades. If I performed poorly or not as well I would have liked, I usually held no grudge against the professor. I rarely believed my grades stemmed from a professor's anger or cruelty. I placed the onus upon myself. For my two lowest grades in undergraduate work, I performed the best I could in those classes and never thought the professors were out to get me.

Students improve when they take responsibility for their actions. They evaluate their performance and adjust accordingly. By contrast, students rarely improve if they believe they are not responsible for their performance. They regard themselves as victims of circumstance, and consequently they do not believe they need to change anything.

Research says, "More than eleven hundred university students were surveyed to determine attitudes toward learning and accountability. Apathy, absenteeism, and grade inflation emerged as contributing to the lack of student accountability."[2]

RELATIONSHIPS WITH PROFESSORS AND EXCUSES

The best students tend to listen to and take advice from their professors. They also show respect for their professors. The best students hardly ever give their professors any trouble and working with them is a joy. The not-so-good students rarely listen to their professors and they tend not to take advice. They also do not show respect for their professors. The not-so-good students take most of the professor's time and they interrupt the class with rude comments or off-the-subject remarks. On one occasion, two students talked in the back of the room and this really distracted me. At the end of the class, I talked to the students because I did not want to embarrass them in front of the entire class. One student apologized but the other denied talking. For the rest of the semester, this student disrupted the class. He never studied and wrote incredibly bad papers. This student performed miserably during his four years in college, and tended to offer excuses for everything. He disrupted more than one class.

Good students need no excuses for their performance. Not-so-good students provide many excuses for their performance. They blame others and circumstances, but rarely themselves, for their grades.

PAY ATTENTION TO DETAIL

In his book *Turning the Thing Around*, two-time Super Bowl–winning coach Jimmy Johnson recounts the night before he coached in his first

conference championship game.[3] Johnson recalls awaking at about 4
A.M. with maps of the resodded field at Candlestick Park staring him in
the face. As Johnson explains, the grounds crew at the stadium needed
to resod significant portions of the field, which were damaged because
of the park's location on San Francisco Bay. Johnson could not sleep because he thought he had overlooked some important detail. Then it hit
him. He took the pictures from his nightstand and called his staff. Johnson and his coaching staff designed plays to take advantage of the conditions. They wanted plays that allowed their players to run on solid turf
whereas the opponents were on the resodded turf, which causes players
to slip easily. At the most critical juncture of the game, Johnson called a
play where his receiver caught the ball on solid ground and the defender
slipped and fell. The play sealed the conference championship for Johnson's team.

The moral of this story is that attention to detail leads to success. The
best students pay attention to detail in their schoolwork. Attention to
detail eliminates proofreading mistakes. Attention to detail adds important information to papers and exams. Attention to detail is a valuable
technique to learn because it is an attribute in any field.

The not-so-good students do not pay attention to detail. Their papers
contain many proofreading mistakes, and they include only the most
basic information. Many not-so-good students simply recopy their
notes into a term paper, whereas the best students, who pay attention to
detail, include information from lectures, required readings, supple-
mentary readings, and outside sources.

THE LESSONS COLLEGE CAN TEACH

When students work hard in college, they learn important life lessons.
Good students understand how to manage their time. Students who
study, attend class, and receive good grades with little supervision develop self-discipline.

Good students learn the importance of paying attention to detail. As
I completed my term papers, for instance, I racked my brain for extra

information to improve them. I wanted to include examples that few other students would provide in order to separate my paper from the rest. I used this information to complement basic material, which most students include in their papers. This process of thinking about unique but important angles and perspectives sharpened my ability to pay attention to detail.

Reflection on the implications of my studies developed my critical thinking skills. College teaches students about substantive lessons, but it also conveys lessons about how to think and write critically. As I tell my students, you should know *what* the Constitution says, *why* the Constitution was written and designed, and *how* government works under this document. Students can Google the contents of the Constitution, but they cannot easily answer *why* and *how* questions about this document simply by reading an article on the Internet or in an encyclopedia. The ability to address *how* and *why* questions facilitates critical thinking and writing skills, which are valuable in any profession. Students acquire critical-thinking and writing skills primarily through reflection of the greater meaning of their subjects (for more on assessment, see chapter 12).

College also teaches students how to establish and reach short- and long-term goals. For instance, reading all the required material for a week represents one short-term goal whereas learning and maintaining a strong overall GPA are long-term goals. One caution about long-term goals: think about them from time to time, but do not focus upon a macroplan on a regular basis. Depression set in whenever I thought too long about the future. Just after I completed my first semester in graduate school, I went to the library and thought about all I needed to accomplish in order to receive a PhD. At that point, thinking about all that I needed to accomplish overwhelmed me. From that moment forward, I thought about the future from time to time, but for the most part I concentrated upon short-term goals.

My collegiate experience also taught me how to overcome losses and disappointments. As I wrote earlier, I rarely tried in high school, so I was not disappointed or surprised by my mediocre grades. By contrast, I tried quite hard in college and on a few occasions the results upset me. The first semester in my junior year was particularly difficult. It felt like I had some assignment due or an exam during each week of the semester. While my GPA rose during my freshmen and sophomore years, it dipped slightly in that semester. I was quite disappointed, but I evaluated what I could have changed and I learned from this semester.

Burns's Rules for Being a Good Student

1. Attend every class
2. Study on a regular basis
3. Do not ask for special treatment
4. View grades as your responsibility
5. Pay attention to detail
6. Take advantage of extra-credit opportunities
7. View grades as impersonal

NOTES

1. For this point, I am indebted to Matthew O. Thomas.

2. Hassel and Lourey, "The Dea(r)th of Student Responsibility."

3. Jimmy Johnson and Ed Hinton, *Turning the Thing Around: Pulling America's Team Out of the Dumps—And Myself Out of the Doghouse* (New York: Hyperion, 1993).

How Parents Can Help Their Children Succeed

Parents Just Don't Understand

When he was the Fresh Prince, Will Smith sang "Parents Just Don't Understand." The song's first verse was "You know parents are the same no matter time nor place. They don't understand that us kids are gonna make some mistakes. So to you, all the kids all across the land, there's no need to argue, parents just don't understand." In this chapter, I try to give parents some information that will help them understand.

I have no children, so I lack a parent's perspective. However, I distinctly remember how my parents handled me when I was in college and I have interacted with several parents during my time as a faculty member. The information in this chapter emanates from these experiences.

IT'S ON YOUR CHILDREN

Your children are responsible for *their* grades. On rare occasions, a student tries hard and still receives a C, D, or even an F in one course but his or her overall GPA will not dip below 2.0. For the most part, if your children get those grades, *they* did something wrong in school. Your children will try to tell you that the professors did not like them or they studied but failed or some other excuse. It has been my experience that students must work hard (or, actually, *not* work hard) to receive a cumulative GPA below 2.0.

I have found many parents who believe the excuses their child makes or assign blame to the university. One time, I received a call from a pretty perturbed parent who wanted to know why her child received low grades. Acting as a diplomat, I said I did not know and that I was *only* the student's adviser. Only the student's adviser?!? The parent thought I should know exactly why her child had performed so poorly. She went on to ask why I did not supervise her child or maintain closer contact with her child. As a diplomat, I tried to explain that I assist and counsel students, but I do not monitor all the activities of students. Even at small colleges, grades are the responsibility of the student, and faculty members can only do so much to assist students. Faculty members do not act as babysitters.

The problem with parents who think like the one I described above is that they do not hold their children accountable for grades. It was fairly clear that this parent blamed *me* in part and the school in part for her child's grades. *Me?* I did not even teach her child. For the most part, students determine their GPAs.

With that said, some professors are curmudgeons or hard-asses who refuse to assign top grades. Other professors may have a personality clash with your child that affects a course grade. My experience is that these are rare cases, which only affect one grade in one course.

In their totality, the semester and overall GPAs reflect effort.

If parents hold colleges and professors accountable for students' grades, then their children will not improve as students. Parents cannot remove accountability from their children. If parents blame others for their children's grades, then students have no reason to improve. I understand that *sometimes* students receive poor grades they did not deserve, but I firmly believe that *for the most part* students get the grades they earn. If parents and students operate with this assumption, then students will improve their performance over time.

CUT THE CORD

Parents need to cut the umbilical cord, as my sister likes to say. When children go to college, parents' responsibility for and oversight of their activities and grades diminishes. As a parent, *you* are not responsible for *your children's* grades. Students, not parents, should inquire about grades and how to improve. Many students know why they received the grades they did, and others come to realize why they earned certain grades. Many students tell me that their GPA was low when they began college because they did not work hard or study. Once these students understood the work necessary to learn in college, their GPAs rose.

I will never forget my first semester in college. This marked the first time I really tried in school. As I noted in chapter 1, I had great difficulty with my Introduction to American Government course. My parents and I have always had a tight bond and an open relationship, and they always made it clear that I was responsible for my grades. In my first semester in college, my father noticed a difference in me. He could tell I was trying, partly because my sister also attended UConn at the time and told him that I studied every night. In a very caring way, my father asked if I wanted him to go see my professor. He thought a meeting among the three of us might help me. I appreciated his interest and the offer, but I understood that I needed to be responsible for my grades. Ultimately, I realized how to improve in this class. The lesson here is that your children will be better off if they figure out how to succeed in college without their parents' direct help. This lesson will help them in life.

What kind of information can parents get from children during the semester? My parents rarely, if ever, asked pointed questions during the semester. They never inquired whether I attended class, went to the library, studied, or other things. They always asked how I was, and this is a good point of departure for a conversation. If your child is stressed about school, sometimes all they want is for you to listen. Other times they may ask for advice. I would listen intently.

Pressing your child is not a good idea. In line with cutting the cord, your children are responsible for themselves in college. You should ask broad questions, such as "How are you doing?" and "Are you eating and sleeping enough?" You should avoid prying questions, including "Where were you last night?" "Why are you not in the library?" and "What is due this week?"

REWARD AND PUNISH

Good grades are a special occasion. Parents should show their children how happy they are with their children's performance. A special meal out, a little party, a hug, or a small celebration can uplift your children's spirits after a good semester. At the very least, parents need to let their children know about how proud they are of their grades.

Parents should punish their children for unacceptable grades. The kind of punishment depends on the child and the parents. I think making children feel uncomfortable is a good way to get a point across, but not all children respond to this kind of punishment.

BE REALISTIC

Like students, parents need to realize that high school and college are different worlds. I have seen too many parents place unrealistic expectations on their students. Parents should demand that their children work hard and do their best. Expectations of a 4.0 GPA or the Dean's List, especially in the first semester, may be unrealistic. Before I went to college, my mother told me she had no expectations about how well I would perform. All she asked was for me to try my hardest and not get too depressed if my grades were average. She encouraged and expected effort, not specific results. Parents should demand effort. Hard work is the most realistic expectation a parent can have of a child.

Research says: 55 percent of students at a major urban Southeastern university who had GPAs between 1.75 and 2.00 warned incoming freshmen to "be ready for freedom and independence."[1]

FREEDOM

Students have unlimited freedom in college. This freedom can be overwhelming for any eighteen-year-old. It is especially overpowering for students who come to college with no experiences of freedom or self-discipline. As your child grows older, you may want to provide more freedom and find ways to develop your child's self-discipline. As a parent's control increases, freedom becomes more difficult for a college student to handle.

Burns's Rules for Parents of College Students

1. Your children are responsible for their grades
2. Inquire about school but do not nag
3. Reward for good grades; punish for bad
4. Set realistic expectations for your children, especially in semester 1

General Tip for Parents of College Students

Provide some freedom for your children before they go to college.

NOTE

1. Commander and Valeri-Gold, "Ideas in Practice."

15

The Most Important Points

If You Work Hard, the Grades Will Come

This book provides plenty of information and many pieces of advice. In this final chapter, I summarize six interrelated and essential pieces of advice that will help you succeed in college.

First, you must work hard. Hard work is nonnegotiable. One time I was speaking with a student who told me she did not perform that well in school. Her grades were a mixture of B's and C's. This student marveled at the performance of her roommate, whose grades were all A's and high B's. I asked this student why her roommate did so well, and she commented on the amount of schoolwork her roommate completed. I explained to her that her roommate's grades were neither a mystery nor the result of sheer intelligence. Instead, her roommate worked hard to earn these grades.

I told this student that she needed to work as hard as her roommate did. She looked at me with a blank stare. The bottom line is that this student did not want to work as hard or dedicate as much time as her roommate did, and her grades reflected her effort. You must work hard in order to succeed in college.

**Summary of the Most Important Advice Offered
in *Success in College***

1. Work hard
2. Make good grades and learning your top priorities
3. Work in advance
4. Use your syllabi to develop a plan to get ahead and stay ahead of your assignments
5. Study on a regular basis
6. Attend all classes

The second point, related to the first, is that learning and good grades must be your priorities. As a student, I made learning and good grades my goals. For the most part, when conflicts arose between school and something else, I chose school. If I had an exam the next day, I would miss the party. If I had a number of papers to write, I would miss a television show or the broadcast of a sporting event.

As a professor, I see students who do not make learning and grades their main concerns. One time, I found out that an intelligent but unmotivated student went to a party instead of working on an assignment that was due the next day. The student waited until the day the assignment was due to start writing essays. I explained to the student how we differed. If I had a conflict between a party and completing an assignment, I would have studied. The student chose the party.

This student could have written the assignment and attended the party had he worked in advance. I worked ahead in order to enjoy both my academic and social lives. This story underscores the next major point of this book, develop a game plan to get ahead and stay ahead of your schoolwork. If that student had mapped out his semester, then he could have lived a balanced life in college.

On rare occasions, I chose some other activity over going to class, but school was always my priority. For instance, I took a bus trip to Washington, DC, during my sophomore year to watch UConn try to clinch the Big East Championship.[1] As a result of the trip, I missed one class. In fact, the class I missed was the only skip I had all semester in that course. After I returned from the bus trip from hell, I made all my classes the next day, and I had planned my activities in advance to work ahead in order to mitigate the effect one miss would exert on my semester. This game represented a special occasion, but I always made school my main concern.

Another student I taught was quite committed to exercise and working out. She rarely missed workout sessions. By contrast, learning and grades were not her priorities. This student rarely approached studying with the same passion she had for working out. She dedicated a portion of her life to exercise, but never made college a priority. She would miss class from time to time, turn in late papers, or complete the assignments at the last moment. If this student had approached studying with the same vigor as exercise, then she would have succeeded in college. Like many others, this student did not make school her top priority.

Another essential activity in college is to study on a regular basis. I cannot tell you what a regular basis is, but on average, I studied five or six days a week. I watch many students do nothing until the week of exams. These students never catch up during the semester. Regular sleeping, eating, and studying patterns will help you flourish during the semester.

Last, but not least important, you must attend all classes. Missing class is a sign that you are not performing well. Few students can miss class and still earn high grades and even fewer can learn without going to class. No matter what, you must attend class on a regular basis. If making class means that you must scrape yourself out of bed, put on baseball hat, and walk like a zombie to class, then do it!

NOTE

1. Georgetown beat UConn that night, 84–64. The next Saturday night, however, UConn clinched a share of the Big East regular season title by beating Boston College, 95–74, and I went to that game. UConn also won the

Big East tournament that year, and I attended all three of those games. They beat Clemson on a last-second shot in the Sweet 16, but lost to Duke on a final-second shot, and I went to both of those games as well. So despite my strict attention to my studies, I led a balanced life by attending UConn basketball games, both in Connecticut and on the road. I managed to get the most out of both experiences.

References

Bogler, Ronit, and Anit Somech. "Motives to Study and Socialization Tactics among University Students." *Journal of Social Psychology* 142, no. 2 (2002): 233–48.

Burns, Peter. *Electoral Politics Is Not Enough: Racial and Ethnic Minorities and Urban Politics.* Albany, NY: SUNY Press, 2006.

Commander, Nannette Evans, and Maria Valeri-Gold. "Ideas in Practice: Letters of Advice from At-Risk Students to Freshmen." *Journal of Developmental Education* 27, no. 1 (2003): 28–30, 32, 34.

"Controlling Inappropriate Classroom Behavior." *Perspective* 19, no. 10 (2004): 3–4.

Doherty, Kathryn M. "Changing Urban Education: Defining the Issues." In *Changing Urban Education,* ed. Clarence N. Stone. Lawrence: University Press of Kansas, 1998.

Enders, Doug. "Crossing the Divide: A Survey of the High School Activities That Best Prepared Students to Write in College." *Clearing House* 75, no. 2 (2001): 62–67.

Ezarik, Melissa. "Be a Real SURVIVOR." *Career World* 30, no. 2 (2001): 6–10.

Glenn, Robert E. "Teach Kids Test-Taking Tactics." *Education Digest* 70, no. 2 (1997): 61–64.

Hassel, Holly, and Jessica Lourey. "The Dea(r)th of Student Responsibility." *College Teaching* 53, no. 1 (2005): 2–13.

Hodge, Trevor V., and Carlton Pickron. "Preparing Students for Success in the Academy." *Black Issues in Higher Education* 21, no. 20 (2004): 130.

Johnson, Jimmy, and Ed Hinton. *Turning the Thing Around: Pulling America's Team Out of the Dumps—And Myself Out of the Doghouse.* New York: Hyperion, 1993.

Kachgal, Mera M., Sunny L. Hansen, and Kevin J. Nutter. "Academic Procrastination Prevention/Intervention: Strategies and Recommendations." *Journal of Developmental Education* 25, no. 1 (2001): 14–21.

Kern, Carolyn W., Nancy S. Fagley, and Paul Miller. "Correlates of College Retention and GPA: Learning and Study Strategies, Testwiseness, Attitudes, and ACT." *Journal of College Counseling* 1, no. 1 (1998): 26–34.

Kirst, Michael W. "The High School/College Disconnect." *Educational Leadership* 62, no. 3 (2004): 51–55.

Kuo, James, Chris Hagie, and Michael T. Miller. "Encouraging College Student Success: The Instructional Challenges, Response Strategies, and Study Skills of Contemporary Undergraduates." *Journal of Instructional Psychology* 31, no. 1 (2004): 60–67.

Loulou, Diane. "How to Study for and Take College Tests." ACCESS ERIC. Washington, DC: Office of Educational Research and Improvement (ED), 1997.

Miley, William M., and Sonia Gonsalves. "Grade Expectations: Redux." *College Student Journal* 38, no. 3 (2004): 327–32.

Parkes, Jay, and Mary B. Harris. "The Purposes of a Syllabus." *College Teaching* 50, no. 2 (2002): 55–61.

Perlmutter, David D. "What Works When Students and Teachers Both Misbehave." *Education Digest* 70, no. 1 (2004): 48–52.

Peter D. Hart Research Associates/Public Opinion Strategies. *Rising to the Challenge: Are High School Graduates Prepared for College and Work? A Study of Recent High School Graduates, College Instructors, and Employers.* Study conducted for Achieve, Inc., February 2005. Available online at www.achieve.org/dstore.nsf/Lookup/pollreport/$file/pollreport.pdf.

Peverly, Stephen T., Karen E. Brobst, Mark Graham, and Ray Shaw. "College Adults Are Not Good at Self-Regulation: A Study on the Relationship of Self-Regulation, Note Taking, and Test Taking." *Journal of Educational Psychology* 95, no. 2 (2003): 335–46.

Sigelman, Lee. "Report of the Editor of the *American Political Science Review*, 2002–2003." *PS: Political Science and Politics* 37 (2004):139–42.

Silvers, Vicki L., and David S. Kreiner, "The Effects of Pre-Existing Inappropriate Highlighting on Reading Comprehension." *Reading Research and Instruction* 36 (Spring 1997): 217–23.

Strunk, William, Jr., and E. B. White. *The Elements of Style*, 3rd ed. Boston: Allyn and Bacon, 2000.

Vermette, Paul. "Improving Understanding and Increasing Grades: 4 Tips for a Fall Freshman at Columbus Day, an Open Letter to My Son at College." *College Student Journal* 34, no. 4 (2000): 611–15.

Williams, Joseph M. *Style: The Basics of Clarity and Grace*, 7th ed. New York: Longman, 1999.

Wilson, Maureen E. "Teaching, Learning, and Millennial Students." *New Directions for Student Services* 106 (Summer 2004): 59–71.

Young, Jeffrey R. "Homework? What Homework?" *Chronicle of Higher Education* 49, no. 15 (2002). Available online at chronicle.com/free/v49/i15/15a03501.htm.

About the Author

Peter Burns is an associate professor of political science at Loyola University New Orleans. He transformed from a mediocre high school student to a member of Phi Beta Kappa who graduated Magna Cum Laude from the University of Connecticut. Since receiving a PhD in government and politics from the University of Maryland in 1999, Burns has taught at Trinity College in Hartford, Connecticut, and Loyola University in New Orleans. Students and faculty have honored Burns with numerous awards for teaching and advising. Burns's research interests include urban affairs, racial and ethnic politics, and public policy. In 1999 the urban section of the American Political Science Association named Burns as one of the first Norton Long Young Scholars for his innovative research. Burns is the author of *Electoral Politics Is Not Enough* (SUNY Press, 2006), which examines the conditions under which white leaders identify and respond to minority interests. His research has appeared in, among other places, the *Journal of Urban Affairs, Urban Affairs Review,* and *Political Science Quarterly.*